Accession no.
36086449

D1587516

ELIZABETH REES
60 QUEEN'S GATE
LONDON SW7
01-581 2005

THE CORPORATE PERSONALITY

AN INQUIRY INTO THE NATURE OF CORPORATE IDENTITY

WALLY OLINS

LIS - LIBRARY

Date	Fund
17/6/09	pgr

Order No.

201564 x

University of Chester

Design Council

The Corporate Personality
an inquiry into the nature of corporate identity

First edition published in the United Kingdom 1978 by
Design Council 28 Haymarket London SW1Y 4SU

Designed by Michael McCarthy
Printed and bound in the United Kingdom by
The Kynoch Press Witton Birmingham

Distributed in the United Kingdom by
Heinemann Educational Books Ltd
48 Charles Street London W1X 8AH

All rights reserved. No part of this publication may be
reproduced, stored in a retrieval system, or transmitted,
in any form or by any means, electronic, mechanical,
photocopying, recording or otherwise, without the prior
permission of the Design Council.

ISBN 0 85072 087 7

©Wally Olins 1978

Contents

Preface

This book investigates the corporate personality. It is concerned with the identity of the company, with the various images that it presents, both haphazard and contrived, and with the reality behind the imagery.

Naturally I write from a particular standpoint. I am a design consultant and I am therefore particularly, although by no means exclusively, concerned with the way the corporation manifests its identity visually, so the book has a bias towards visual matters.

The book is written for people who are interested in why companies behave in the way they do and about how their behaviour relates to their appearance. It's about how the appearance of an organisation can be controlled, and how this can make the company more effective, more profitable and a better place to work in. It's also about how the company relates to society and what society expects from the company. The book deals with the difference between a brand identity and a corporate identity and it explains how to develop an identity programme—how long it takes, what to do and what not to do, how to do it, in what order, and how much it all costs.

I have aimed the book primarily at managers, particularly those who are curious about their own environment and those who may be involved in shaping their company's identity or those of its brands. I am thinking here of executives in general and technical management, production, engineering and finance, as well as marketing, advertising and PR.

The book will, I hope, also interest young people who are thinking of going into business, and perhaps even those who are antagonistic to it because they find its atmosphere unpleasant. Even if I can't change the atmosphere, I may at least be able to explain how it got that way. And because the book is largely about the things that we all see I hope it will also interest anybody else who is involved in architecture and design.

Many of the examples relate to experiences that I have had or that people I know have had. Since much of my working background has been in Europe, in which I include Britain, many of my examples come from there. For this I apologise to non-European readers. Where corporate identity touches on sociological problems or there seem to be appropriate historical analogies I deal with these, but the book has no sociological or historical pretensions.

The book is, for better or worse, not so much a summary of what I know about corporate identity—the business in which I have been working for many, perhaps too many, years—as a distillation of the opinions and experiences of Wolff Olins, the company for which I work.

Many people have helped me with developing ideas for the book. I should like particularly to thank my colleagues Terence Griffin and Michael Wolff, Peter Gorb of the London Business School, Robert Heller, Editor of *Management Today,* and Jacques Bouvard of Conseil et Entreprise in Paris, all of whom read the book and gave me much helpful advice, a little of which I took.

Finally, I am most grateful to Renate Haubrock, who bore much of the burden of preparing the book by typing the manuscript several times and involving herself in a great deal of the research.

In spite of the help I received I need hardly say, however, that I take full responsibility for the style of the book, such as it is, the content and, most particularly, for the errors and omissions. Although so far as I know all the factual information I have put down is accurate at the time of writing, things change so quickly in the business world that by the time you read what I have written some of the current events may have become history.

Wally Olins

Introduction

Corporate identity is now a fashionable and much used tool of top management. Many companies anxious to create an image or to change it employ design consultants to work on their image problems.

These designers, after an investigation, sometimes come up with a new corporate name and usually with a new way of writing it. They produce a new symbol and new colours to identify the corporation. These graphic devices are applied to the company's stationery and its vehicles. They are put up as signs on buildings, on packaging and as sign-offs on advertising. A thick book of carefully drawn and detailed pictures, called the design manual, is produced and the job is done. The company has its new image and the designers move on.

That is how most companies and most design consultants interpret corporate design. Naturally, the larger design companies and their bigger clients wrap it up so that it sounds more sophisticated and clever, but that is what most corporations want when they carry out a corporate image programme and it is what most design companies collude with them in providing.

Not surprisingly perhaps, after 25 years or so, a cloud is beginning to grow over the corporate identity business. Businessmen are starting to ask themselves whether this is really another case where the Emperor has no clothes. Is all this fuss about corporate identity and image just a lot of nonsense about symbols, colours and a few bits of type? If these doubts grow the corporate design business will be in trouble and I and a lot of my colleagues will be out of work.

The truth of the matter is that some sense of identity is natural to any society. Industrial organisations, as they get more complex, have to develop a culture that enables people working within them to understand one another. This culture is often best projected visually; it provides a signalling mechanism. The visual projection of a culture not only helps internal cohesion, but it plays a large part in showing the outside world what the company is like and how it can be expected to behave.

This book deals with the reality of the corporate identity problem. I start by explaining the basic human need to project an identity; I go on to discuss when, where and how this need emerged in industry and commerce. I then deal with some of the manifestations of identity that occur among nations. The book then moves on to its ma theme—the problems of corporate identity for intricate a complicated businesses in modern society. It deals with issue from various points of reference: with the proble the corporation dominated by one powerful personality; with the corporation that has expanded both horizontally and vertically to such an extent that it is no longer clearly classifiable as being in any one group of businesses. It also deals with structural problems in a company—with the differences between an identity for various brands and one for the whole corporation. It deals with the relationship between the corporation and society as a whole and the corporation and the people who work for it. It talks about names of different kinds, how they emerge, how they are used and misused.

The book takes examples from a variety of industries— food, aircraft, banking, automobiles and many more—and from many countries. All of these examples highlight problems of corporate identity.

The book then deals with the design consultants, what they do, where they come from and how they got there. It talks about individual consultants, what they can do, what they can't do, how they operate and how they charge. It also explains how they should be used most effectively.

In the final section of the book I explain how to carry out a corporate identity programme, the various stages through which such a programme moves and the opportunities and problems that occur at each point.

I believe that corporate identity when used properly— that is thoroughly, sensitively, carefully and above all permanently—is vital to any successful business or industrial activity.

The corporate identity business, as a business, is still very young, and if it contains shysters, charlatans and incompetents, they are no higher a proportion than exists in any other trade. It might be more charitable to think that all of us are still, as yet, only serving our apprenticeship at this complex and difficult activity.

Chapter 1
Some definitions and some history
William and the Outlaws, the Jolly Roger,
the Roman Catholic Church,
and the Great Northern, Great Eastern, Great Western
and a few more railways.

Corporate identity was not invented, together with management by objectives, cash flow control techniques and other management consultancy parlour games, some time around 1953. Its history is ancient, curious and, for the most part, honourable. It derives from a study of the way people behave when they form groups. From the family unit through school and university to the factory or office, people always work in groups. Corporate behaviour is what results when people get together to form such a group.

Groups always develop an identity, a personality and a behaviour pattern of their own, different from and greater than the sum of the personalities involved.

Schoolteachers have a lot of experience of this. Classes vary considerably in personality, ability and the will to work. When a teacher says, 'This year's fourth form is rowdier than last year's', he doesn't mean that everybody in the class is worse behaved, but that the general level of behaviour is worse. The rowdy atmosphere may have been created by only one or two young people, but their personalities have been powerful enough to affect the whole.

When the group is a nation the identity becomes much more obvious. National patterns of behaviour—what people call national character—are very plain. Americans, Italians and Germans have recognisable national characteristics even though not every American, Italian or German behaves in the same way.

'Visitors to the United States', says William R Brock, Professor of History at the University of Glasgow, in a paper on Americanism (*The United States,* edited by Dennis Welland), 'are frequently impressed by the outward show and symbols of conscious nationalism. Children are taught to salute the flag, and it is flown by private individuals to demonstrate their patriotism. The word "American" is used with a wealth of overtones, so that to describe oneself or a custom or an institution as "American" is to claim a whole set of positive values . . .

'The "all-American" boy has become something of a joke, but it is a character which most American parents covet for their sons. Conversely, to be "un-American" is not to be merely foreign or unfamiliar but dangerous, immoral, subversive and deluded. Fourth of July orations are the classic expressions of American patriotism, but hyperbole is not confined to these rhetorical exercises and to foreign ears the discourse of public men seems to be marked to an extraordinary degree by appeals to the special character and destiny of the American people.'

Certainly nationality has a profound effect on how we dress, what we eat, on our habits and, above all, on the way we behave. It is said that you can tell a man's nationality on holiday by the way he puts up a tent. Germans, French and English are never so conscious of their own national identities as when they are on holiday, happily treading all over the Spaniard's identity on the Costa del Sol.

Most groups want to make an impression as a coherent unit on the various parts of society with which they deal. Groups of children may call themselves the Red Fang or Bloody Hand Gang for precisely the same reasons that adult secret societies gave themselves romantic and mysterious names. Gavrelo Princip, the young Serbian student who assassinated the Archduke Franz Ferdinand and his wife Sophie at Sarajevo in July 1914, thereby precipitating the First World War, was influenced by a secret society called the Black Hand. Its leader was the head of Serbian Military Intelligence, Colonel Dimitrijevic, who called himself Apis. Organisations like this want to foster their own elitism and to appear mysterious to those outside their circle.

"It makes one want to go off an' be a robber," continued William.

From names it's only a small step to signs, secret or otherwise, heraldry, uniforms and all the other trappings of visual identity. The group, whether it's as small and primitive as Richmal Crompton's William and his Outlaws or a sophisticated multinational enterprise like IBM, uses all the visual means available to it to reinforce its own identity and to make this identity clear to all the different groups with which it deals.

But the name and the visual identity chosen by the group tend to encapsulate—with imagery—what the group holds to be its essential raison d'être. The schoolboys' Red Fang Gang exists as an organisation for terrorising all fatties and wets; IBM's style locks it firmly into the world of modern business technology.

So the imagery serves to project to the outside world and reflect to the group itself what the subject in hand is to be. The Jolly Roger proclaims piracy, reminding the crew of the bad behaviour that is expected of them.

Visual identity, therefore, is a part of the deeper identity of the group, the outward sign of inward commitment, serving to remind it of its real purpose.

The world has a rich and entertaining history of visual identity. It is intrinsic to any society, at any place and at any time. So while it would not be appropriate in this book, which is concerned primarily with the identities of big corporations, to carry out a detailed study of pre-Industrial Revolution corporate identities, it is worth looking at some outstanding examples of identity from the past, simply in order to get some kind of perspective.

Hugh Trevor-Roper in his *Princes and Artists*, which he subtitles *Patronage and Ideology at four Habsburg Courts 1517-1633*, explains how the Habsburgs used artists in the sixteenth and seventeenth centuries to project a particular view of their rule:

'. . . at the time of the Renaissance the princely courts took over . . . both the product and direction of art and made it serve their propaganda and their prestige.'

In Florence, at an earlier period, the Medicis were even more conscious that art encapsulated the prestige and aspirations of the state in a powerful and appealing fashion. A great deal of the world's art, many of its finest buildings and much of its music have been produced as part of some overall propaganda exercise.

Spiritual authorities were much more consistent than temporal rulers in their use of art for indoctrination purposes. The Roman Catholic Church found out about the effect of visual identity a very long while ago. The corporate identity activities of the Church have been continuous, unremitting and, on balance, highly successful.

The Church has always paid the closest possible attention to its identity. From the very early days it has developed rituals, introduced special clothing, and used complex and impressive titles within a carefully ordered naming structure. It has erected buildings of considerable sophistication and used many symbols, all collectively designed to make a massive impact on the various audiences with which it deals. In the Middle Ages when the Church needed recruits it made itself attractive to intelligent youngsters. It needed to impress the temporal powers and it did so by the use of titles, uniforms, and a rich, complex and mysterious ritual that took place within vast, sophisticated, technologically advanced buildings— the cathedrals. It needed to impress the mass of the laity and it did so by claiming to be and looking separate, but by penetrating deeply into the fabric of their lives.

The Roman Catholic Church followed a similar path in terms of its identity to some other major religions. It did not work out a visual identity programme consciously as part of a deliberate strategy.

The Church has always intuitively recognised the power of identity and at different times, for different

A Dominican, a Jesuit and a Franciscan of about 1650

reasons and in different ways it has developed what we could call identity programmes. It has rarely abandoned an existing style or pattern of behaviour. When a new movement or activity becomes appropriate the Church simply adds it to the existing collection. So Franciscans can coexist with Jesuits and the splendour of Renaissance Rome can be seen alongside earlier austerities.

Naturally the Church was not alone in its corporate identity development. In mediaeval Europe the entire temporal feudal system that parallelled the Church used intricate imagery to project itself.

The mediaeval commercial world, however, was so rudimentary that visual imagery didn't play much of a role. The Guild and trade signs were used as much to assist illiterates as to foster any spirit of togetherness or make an outward show. Marks, seals, letters of credit and the markings on other financial documents served in a subsidiary way to underline the identity of an organisation, but their prime purpose was to guarantee credit.

Among the largest commercial houses of the pre-industrial era were the companies trading with the East. The English, Dutch and other East Indian companies were in a semi-monopoly position. Their representatives were so clearly distinguished from those among whom they traded by the colour of their skins, their language, their clothes

A European at a Mogul court

and the way they lived as to make any other distinguishing features redundant—although of course their soldiers wore uniforms. The goods they brought back were either straightforward commodities like silk and cotton cloth or so specialised that they didn't need extra identification.

We have to reach the Industrial Revolution before we find commercial and industrial organisations that were sufficiently large and complex to warrant the development of modern principles of identity.

The first phase of the Industrial Revolution had little real effect on the growth and organisation of industry as we know it today. It is true that some firms had powerful and idiosyncratic personalities, largely derived from their founders, but these were craft companies making products that were unmistakably their own. Josiah Wedgwood's eighteenth-century factory, which he so carefully and deliberately called Etruria, on the basis that his products were in some degree derived from Etruscan design, is perhaps the extreme example of this and in some ways, allowing for the difference in period, it has similarities to Rosenthal's twentieth-century factories and methods.

It was the second phase of the Industrial Revolution, however, the age of coal, iron and railway construction, that led to the development of huge, complex enterprises that couldn't be controlled in the traditional way and for which new techniques had to be developed.

The construction and management of railway systems led to problems that were very much bigger than anything that had ever been attempted before. All the requirements of modern management emerged virtually at the same time—marketing, employee relations, finance and accountancy, technology, planning and scheduling.

E J Hobsbawm, the eminent economic historian, writes in *Industry and Empire:*

'In effect, by 1850 the basic English railway network was already more or less in existence . . . It transformed the speed of movement—indeed of human life—from one measured in single miles per hour to one measured in scores of miles per hour, and introduced the notion of a gigantic, nation-wide, complex and exact interlocking routine symbolised by the railway time-table (from which all the subsequent "time-tables" took their name and inspiration). It revealed the possibilities of technical progress as nothing else had done, because it was both more advanced than most other forms of technical activity and omnipresent . . . by 1850 the railways had reached a standard of performance not seriously improved upon until the abandonment of steam in the mid-twentieth century, their organisation and methods were on a scale unparalleled in any other industry, their use of novel and science-based technology (such as the electric telegraph) unprecedented. They appeared to be several generations ahead of the rest of the economy, and indeed "railway" became a sort of synonym for ultra-modernity in the 1840s, as "atomic" was to be after the Second World War. Their sheer size and scale staggered the imagination and dwarfed the most gigantic public works of the past.'

The railway constructors employed thousands of men in construction activities in every continent.

Elsewhere, in *The Age of Capital,* Hobsbawm writes: 'Neither can we fail to be moved by the hard men in top hats who organised and presided over these vast transformations of the human landscape—material and spiritual. Thomas Brassey (1805-70), who at times employed 80,000 men on five continents, was merely the most celebrated of these entrepreneurs . . .'

Many groups owned railways in more than one country. The interests of the company and the nation were not always seen to coincide. The multinational arrived in full flower in the 1850s.

Inevitably, competitive railway companies made determined, and at times even exaggerated, efforts to project their own independent identities. Sir John Betjeman, in *London's Historic Railway Stations* says: 'The individuality of the great companies was expressed in styles of architecture, typography and liveries of engines and carriages, even down to the knives and forks and crockery used in refreshment rooms and dining cars.'

The age of corporate identity as we know it, for better or worse, had arrived.

Complicated organisations bringing together people with different social backgrounds in frameworks that demanded the use of related skills could not have been successful unless standards of behaviour were laid down and then heavily emphasised. The railways wanted their employees to adopt a common attitude towards one another and towards the travelling public. They had a particular need to be clearly known and recognised far away from their home base. Each general manager wanted his own company to be seen as the best and his employees to behave appropriately. The companies expressed this intention through a common style in their buildings, liveries, typography, uniforms, and in the quality and appearance of their equipment. In this they anticipated the airlines by a hundred years.

What makes the study of railway identities so fascinating is that in Britain, where it all began and where they developed fastest, they were all so different from one another. Here is Betjeman again:

'The Midland favoured Gothic, and so, in a less expensive way, did the Great Eastern. The Great Western remained its strong Gooch-and-Brunel self. Greek learning dominated the London and North Western. The Great Northern went in for a reliable homeliness rather than beauty.

'Each of these railways had devoted and loyal staffs proud of the line, jealous of its rights and conscious of its dignity.'

The Midland Railway was the line for comfort rather than speed. It introduced dining cars in the very early days and its rolling stock was always particularly agreeable to travel on, although rarely quite as fast as its competitors. St Pancras Station, its scarlet brick terminal in London,

JOHN GAY

The Midland's St Pancras   *The Great Northern's King's Cross*

was much grander than next door King's Cross, London terminal of the rival Great Northern Railway. The Great Northern was, as Betjeman says, 'noted more for its trains than its buildings.' The Midland put Sir Gilbert Scott's fantastical Gothic palace in front of Barlow's magnificent engine shed, but the Great Northern's workmanlike King's Cross was designed by Lewis Cubitt with the minimum delay, cost and fuss. The attitude of the two next door neighbour companies could hardly have been more different. In all the things that mattered—where they invested their money, what they cared about, the nature of their technology—there were marked differences.

Their contrasting personalities lingered on even when both companies had been merged with others to form, in the case of the Midland, the London Midland and Scottish Railway and, in the case of the Great Northern, the London and North Eastern.

The greatest and most idiosyncratic railway of all was the Great Western—Brunel's railway. With its broad gauge track, beautifully maintained rolling stock, and the slightly strange visual character of its engines, many of which were designed by perhaps the greatest Victorian locomotive engineer, Daniel Gooch, it developed an elitism that has almost managed to survive death itself.

The Western Region is still, one is told, the most punctual and efficient on British Rail. The latest high speed train has been introduced on Brunel's and Gooch's old line between London and the West.

At the same time and for the same reasons as the railway companies developed their identities, the world's shipping lines began to develop theirs. The Cunard, the White Star, the Norddeutsche Lloyd, the Hamburg Amerika, the Compagnie Générale Transatlantique were all formed and developed in the great age of steam.

Chapter 2
Different ways of doing it
Hitler, Speer, the CIA, the Guide Michelin, Unilever and some others.

There is no more dramatic and truly horrific example of corporate identity at its most glittering, powerful and hypnotic than that of the Third Reich. All the Fascist movements used an elaborate choreography of torchlight processions, uniforms, martial music and bogus historical symbols, but in Hitler's Germany this, like everything else, was taken to extremes.

Hitler faced a classic identity problem, both internally and externally, when he came to power in 1933. He wanted to rebuild German self-confidence after defeat in war, Versailles, occupation, inflation and the slump. He wanted Germans to work together and with the Nazi Party. He wanted them to believe in him and the strength of his leadership. He wanted them to do what he told them and to want to do it. Above all, he wanted Germany to be admired and feared in the outside world.

As part of his technique to mould Germany and the Germans, Hitler used all the paraphernalia of corporate identity. Goebbels was made responsible for propaganda or, as we might put it today, public relations. Education, the arts, sport, industry, journalism were all controlled in one way or another by his political machine.

All the grubby nineteenth-century detritus of racial superiority produced by de Gobineau, Houston Stewart Chamberlain and others was raked up and re-presented in a new and seductive form.

The Hitler Youth, the Auto Union and Mercedes Benz racing cars, the 1936 Olympic Games, the Autobahnen, the virulently anti-semitic newspaper *Völkischer Beobachter* and the SS were all different manifestations of the identity programme of the Reich.

The whole thing was developed and packaged in brown and black and red and white. It was given a symbol, uniforms and flags. Albert Speer, Hitler's architect and later his minister of production, was put in charge of corporate identity.

Hitler was very interested in architecture and the arts, as Speer tells us in his book *Inside the Third Reich*. It is clear from what he says that much of the visual symbolism that the Nazis used was tired and old and had been around for a long time. The swastika, a so-called Aryan symbol of good luck, had been used by the Freikorps in the 1920s, as well as in situations as diverse as the markings of the Finnish Air Force and the covers of Rudyard Kipling's books. It had arrived in Northern Europe circuitously through its association with the Aryan Hindus. Some of

A Finnish Air Force fighter of the 1920s

The symbol on Rudyard Kipling's books

the visual symbolism that the Nazis used was entirely new, however, and must have been consciously developed.

Speer is quite clear that Hitler used him deliberately during the time that he was his architect to create manifestations of power and strength:

'Hitler liked to say that the purpose of his building was to transmit his time and its spirit to posterity. Ultimately, all that remained to remind men of the great epochs of history was their monumental architecture, he would philosophise . . . Our architectural works should also speak to the conscience of a future Germany centuries from now.'

Later in the book Speer says that Hitler made him wear uniform in public, together with others:

'his doctor, the photographer, even the director of Daimler-Benz had already received a uniform.'

Speer speaks of his role in co-ordinating the visual aspects of the Nazi identity:

'I too had a strenuous time of it at Nuremberg, having been made responsible for all the buildings in which Hitler would appear during the course of the rally. As "chief decorator" ... I dearly loved flags and used them wherever I could ... I found it a boon that the swastika flag Hitler had designed proved more amenable to these uses than a flag divided into three stripes of colour ... Quite often I added gold ribbons to the flag to intensify the effect of the red.'

Later in the same chapter Speer writes:

'By this time I thoroughly admired the art with which Hitler would feel his way during his rallies until he had found the point to unleash the first great storm of applause. I was by no means unaware of the

demagogic element; indeed I contributed to it myself by my scenic arrangements.'

Speer. was commissioned to build a new stadium in Nuremberg, to create the choreography for the party rallies, to redesign Berlin and ultimately to redesign Linz.

The Third Reich not only used colours, symbols, buildings, uniforms and signs in order to manipulate its identity, but it also went so far as to use body movements— the outstretched arm—and speech—the 'Heil Hitler' greeting.

The Hitler period burns itself into the consciousness through its aggressive, and by association horrifying, visible manifestations. To get a measure of how powerful the Nazi identity was, try and think of Nazi Germany without it—no uniforms, no swastika, no Heil Hitler, no outstretched arm.

Not many people have had Hitler's opportunities to launch a corporate identity, nor have they seized it with such maniacal enthusiasm. To find another example on such a large scale with such a massive impact both internally and externally is not easy.

What we are looking for is a highly institutionalised society with special clothing, ways of speech, body movements, buildings, vehicles, food and way of life. The armed forces perhaps come nearest.

The American Army, for instance, has its own buildings, uniforms, equipment, typography, signs and all the other lumber that goes to make up the visible manifestations of a corporate identity. Like all armies it uses particular body movements and idiosyncratic forms of address.

What is particularly interesting about the US Army is that its visual influence has been so pervasive that it has affected all its allies.

The English public schools—which are, in fact, privately owned and maintained institutions competing on a kind of private enterprise system with state education—are also examples of institutions with a self-conscious and highly developed corporate identity.

The most famous of the English public schools is Eton College. The familiar signs are readily identifiable: the clothes and the private language are mildly eccentric; the architecture is distinctive and dominating. All of these things help to engender a feeling of elitism amongst the boys, to emphasise the school's apartness and, by inference, its superiority.

HOMER SYKES

The Fourth of June at Eton College

It may seem a far cry from the gentle and anachronistic elitism of Eton and the terrifying hysteria of Nazi Germany to the bustling commercial world of the United Parcels Service of Greenwich, Connecticut, but in fact UPS, in its wholehearted dedication to getting the job done in a disciplined and ordered way, shares a number of characteristics with the other examples, at least in terms of the way it uses imagery.

UPS is dedicated to the task, simple in concept but complicated in detail, of moving small parcels over the United States in the shortest possible time and in the most economical fashion.

UPS is very big; probably the largest independent parcel moving service in the world. It has many thousands of vehicles and employees and its main competitor is the US Post Office. To do its job efficiently it needs to train its people to work in a particular way and to obey certain rules. It wants to do this in a manner that creates the maximum goodwill, both internally and externally.

UPS is idiosyncratic. It is owned by its managers, who are dispersed geographically within a large number of small units. Unless standards are laid down carefully and maintained with rigour, local variations in performance will throw the whole machine out of gear.

UPS had to develop an intricate programme in order to motivate its people and keep their standards up. It practises elitism through a private language and complex symbolism. Delivery trucks or vans, for example, are called package cars. These package cars, and indeed the entire fleet, are specially adapted to suit UPS' requirements. All vehicles appear in a standard brown livery, the name of the manufacturer is removed and certain modifications are made to most of the bodies to disguise the vehicles' origins. No UPS vehicle has Mack, GMC, Chevrolet, Dodge or Ford badges on it. All UPS package cars are washed daily. According to the American *Commercial Car Journal* everything is standardised and coded: a flat tyre is a 471, a road service call is a 386. What most transport people would call a break-bulk terminal or major distribution centre is, in the world of UPS, called a hub; what you or I might call a branch is an operating centre and every package is a shipment. The man who drives the package car and delivers the shipment is a parcelman.

UPS, with its own language, uniforms and specially adapted vehicles is in many ways a private world, carefully developed with the intention of making people behave predictably.

All of these examples have a lot in common. First, all the organisations we have looked at try to inculcate a permanent attitude and set of standards in those who belong. Second, they have the opportunity to do this because they influence the manner and style in which the group behaves and the environment in which it lives. Third, they are thorough in the use of the opportunities available to them. Fourth, they are anxious to impress the world outside with their homogeneity and strength.

It doesn't always follow that an organisation influencing the behaviour and thought processes of those who belong to it will want to make a public display of the fact. Many organisations of this kind do not wish to project their personalities to the outside world. No doubt the indefatigable employees of the *Guide Michelin* who tramp around the roads of Europe destroying their digestion so that the rest of us can eat decently are in this category. We must also presume that the US secret service, the CIA, is not anxious to make a public exhibition of itself.

In the case of the CIA and the Michelin inspectors a visible manifestation of corporate identity would be harmful since their work has a clandestine or at least semi-clandestine character. But all organisations of this kind are not clandestine. The Jesuits are not, for instance, and neither is Unilever in the world of industry and commerce. Unilever is an interesting example of an organisation with a powerful corporate identity but a low external profile.

Unilever is an Anglo-Dutch company. It is one of the world's largest corporations and it has operations in most countries of the world. In almost all of these countries it has a number of companies—a soap company, a foods company, a toiletries company and a transport company, for example. Usually these companies have different names. Some of these names, like Lever Brothers or Lever Sunlicht, relate to the corporate name, Unilever. Others, however, like Elbe or Nordsee or Wall's do not.

Most, although not all, of Unilever's activities are in branded goods. Unilever companies are not usually well known, although their brands are. So there is a three-tier system—the brand, the company and the corporation.

In addition, in many countries Unilever has a national management—a German Unilever or a Swedish Unilever—that in some ways presents a Unilever face to the business, industrial and commercial community of the host country. But inevitably, for the most part, Unilever is perceived through its brands—Omo, Lux, Rama and so on.

From the outside then, although Unilever makes no attempt to hide, it isn't all that easy to see. There are few clear outward and visible signs of its presence.

Nairn Williamson Ltd Elida Gibbs Ltd Lever Brothers van den Berg light Unilever Indonesia Apollo GmbH La Roche aux Fees SA A/S Denofa og Clynol Ltd Union De g Co Industries Lever Lever Nippon Lever Industrie artog's Levensmiddelen NV T Wall & Sons Ltd td Hindustan Lever Ltd Birds Eye Foods Ltd n Ltd ver Iberica SA Turun Saippua Lever Asociados Lever Broth Sunlight Vinolia Industrials Gessy Lever Sunlicht Mac Fisheries Ltd Sunlight AG Paul a Lever Brothers Pty Ltd John West Foods Ltd Batchelors Foods Ltd Lever SA Mattessons Meats

TIMOTHY QUALLINGTON

The three levels of Unilever — the corporation, some companies and some brands

And yet, despite all these layers, Unilever has a very powerful corporate identity. Unilever executives from Germany, France, India, Britain or Spain are all very carefully recruited and trained. Unilever, like most elitist organisations, likes to catch them young. It tends to recruit its potential managers straight from university and then to train them in its own careful, in some ways gentle, and very effective way. It rarely recruits managers from other organisations, although it will take on specialists.

Unilever's great strength is in its training systems. It teaches people not only how to be good at marketing and other specialised techniques, but also how to be good Unilever people. There is a Unilever way of behaving, a Unilever way of getting on with other people, and a Unilever style of doing business that anybody who has ever dealt with Unilever recognises.

The sophistication of the indoctrination methods is such that a Unilever man's individual personality and national character are not blunted. It is as though another dimension has been added, a kind of Unileverness.

Unileverness is best summed up in the word moderation, the quality of being reasonable. Not necessarily a characteristic that ensures success, but certainly one that inhibits failure.

One senior Unilever executive described the organisation to me as the best men's club in the world. He identified two systems of communication, the official and the grapevine.

Since Unilever senior executives meeting one another over the years on the never-ending series of training courses that are characteristic of the Unilever method form an unofficial grapevine system of communication, there is obviously a lot in what my Unilever friend says. If there is one thing the Unilever system ensures, it is that wherever there is a Unilever company anywhere in the world it will behave predictably, in a way the rest of Unilever will understand. Its national characteristics will remain sufficiently powerful for it to have a clear grasp of local marketing, political and commercial requirements, but its Unilever characteristics will nevertheless always be sufficiently strong for it to get the best from its international connections.

Unilever seems to believe that the best way that it can be an effective organisation is by having powerful internal disciplines and predictable behaviour patterns, and by keeping its head down and minding its own business so far as the outside world is concerned.

Despite its coyness, Unilever has a readily recognisable and somewhat idiosyncratic personality—as do the other examples we have looked at so far in this chapter. But most organisations in most places doing most things don't have very strong personalities. They are influenced by other organisations which they emulate with a certain lack of conviction.

In the commercial and industrial world the so-called 'house style' has emerged over the past 20 or 30 years as a standard fitment in the big company package. Naturally, companies with no strong natural identity of their own have latched on to this, just as they have latched on to so many other fashionable techniques. Companies with no real individual character have been very ready to adopt the fashionable visual style of the day. That is the main reason why, over the last generation, so many major companies have adopted more or less identical programmes.

These companies each had perfectly good reasons for developing an identity programme: they needed to make customers recognise their products as different from and, if possible, superior to those of competitors; they needed to persuade financial institutions to offer them money; they needed to attract the best people to work for them; they needed to persuade local authorities that they were good neighbours. They were aware of a need to project themselves internally and externally. It's just that what came out wasn't very interesting or special. It didn't say anything about the company.

Very many of the corporate identity programmes produced for the world's major companies—Exxon, Siemens, BICC, Westinghouse, RCA, Canadian National, British Steel, BASF, TWA—fall into this category. We will examine some of them in more detail later; meanwhile it's important that we should realise that the category exists and understand why it has emerged.

Finally in this sweeping general survey, we should take a look at those organisations that do nothing about projecting their identity, which are not necessarily even conscious that they have such a thing, and which wouldn't recognise it if they saw it in the street.

This category includes the vast majority of organisations of all kinds. Small homogeneous groups led by powerful people operating in narrow or well defined bands of activity don't need any outward and visible manifestations, signs or symbols to show themselves, or indeed the world outside, who they are; who and what they are emerges from what they do. But organisations that don't make much of their identity or their personality generally appear the same as most other organisations doing the same thing. In the absence of a distinct or carefully defined identity they take on the characteristics of the nearest related big identity.

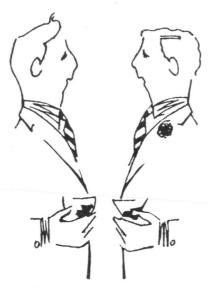

'I'm with Shell, or is it ICI?'

So in a sense any Paris greengrocer or New York hamburger joint seems much like another. Similarly, in industrial terms, one Midlands engineering company in Britain seems much like another. 'They're a typical Midlands engineering company' conveys a specific set of visual and emotional and, quite frequently, commercial, impressions too. 'They're a typical German engineering company' conveys another set of impressions. The French, with their craze for classification, have invented a three-letter word for the huge bag of undistinguishable smaller and medium sized companies: they call them 'PME' —Petites et Moyennes Entreprises.

This kind of organisation, which has no conscious identity and no clearly emergent personality, is at the other end of the spectrum from those we first looked at. In those everything was controlled, even the thoughts, clothes, food, buildings, furniture, body movements and forms of speech. In the second type of organisation nothing is controlled.

Chapter 3
A short diversion into national characteristics
The two Germanys, India, Pakistan, Bangladesh, some of the
new African states and a few other countries that consciously
mould their identities.

Berlin is one of the most curious cities in the world,
largely because there are two of it—East and West. They are
strikingly different and might be a thousand miles apart.

While West Berlin is a prosperous place full of
advertising signs, traffic jams and fashionably dressed
people, jumbled up with the usual urban squalor, East
Berlin is a rather drab capital with spacious, empty
boulevards flanked by anonymous buildings that almost
always turn out to be workers' flats. It has lots of troops and
police and large numbers of adequately dressed people.
East Berlin looks different from West Berlin and it has a
completely different atmosphere. It even seems to smell
different because the tobacco and the petrol have a
different flavour. Although the people are really much the
same, the clothes, hair styles and make-up of West Berliners
make them seem more attractive to us than East Berliners.
Certainly East and West Berlin have a totally different feel,
a different personality and a very different identity from
each other. Strangely enough, one of the few things that
have remained the same in the two cities is the name—both
still call themselves Berlin.

On the other hand, the two Berlins share certain
things—language, food and weather for example. What
they share above all, however, is their Berlinness.

The same is true of Germany as a whole. Although
many West Germans feel that the two Germanys are
growing farther apart because they have been developing
in such different cultural, economic, political, moral and
spiritual climates, each still has a very powerful German
quality. This German-ness simply expresses itself
differently in each case.

The German writer Hans Magnus Enzensberger,
quoted in *The Economist* of 26 February 1977, has this to
say on the subject:
'We belong to two parts of a whole which does not
exist; two parts, each of which denies being a part and
each presents itself in the name of the whole . . . This
condition is regarded as at once temporary and
definitive.'

One Germany is no less German than the other. Both
have latched on to new identities, the one as a prosperous,

democratic, materialist society; the other as a socialist, atheist people's republic. Both have done so with a wholehearted enthusiasm, vigour and efficiency that the rest of the world regards as characteristically German.

It is German enthusiasm and thoroughness that have made East and West Germany outstandingly successful examples of their very different political systems. German singleminded enthusiasm has built up East German sporting achievements to be the finest, for the size of the country, in the world. The same German drive has rebuilt the West German economy so that it is the strongest in Europe. Even though they look so different from each other, East and West German cities look German. The paradox is at its most acute in Berlin.

West Berlin   *East Berlin*

So there are two German images presenting two faces of the same personality. Neither is a counterfeit. It's just a bit strange that Chemnitz has become Karl-Marx-Stadt while East Berlin is still called Berlin.

In other places where there has been a dramatic change in the political structure, particularly in former colonial territories, names sometimes get thrown out at the same time and with the same lack of ceremony as do the statues of former rulers. In some countries totally new names have to be coined. Some places undergo changes of name and accompanying changes of identity with bewildering speed.

In 1946 there was no Pakistan and all of what we now call India, Pakistan and Bangladesh was called India. Then Pakistan was formed. Owing to the curious geographical disposition of Muslims in the subcontinent, Pakistan had two wings, over a thousand miles apart. West Pakistan was formed out of North Western India, and East Pakistan was carved out of Bengal.

The East Pakistanis, who were of Bengali origin, had nothing much in common with the West Pakistanis, who were mainly Sindhis, Pathans and Punjabis, except their religion and a fear of India. When the Bengalis found that they disliked being tied to their western brothers in Islam just as they had resented the tie with India, that was the beginning of the end of East Pakistan. There was a war and the country gained independence for the second time. It changed its name again too—to Bangladesh.

So the Muslim Bengali inhabitants of Bengal have changed the name of their country twice in the past 30 years. Bangladesh is of course now a fully-fledged country. It has a new flag, a new national anthem and, of course, a new

Bangladesh Biman—the international airline of Bangladesh

airline. For a time it had two new armies—an official one and an unofficial one—an air force, a navy and, after the ritual coup, a newish government.

The Hindu Bengalis of West Bengal are racially the same as the Bangladeshi Muslims. They speak the same language, eat more or less the same food and have similar attitudes to life. During the 30 years that have proved so tempestuous for what we now call Bangladesh, formerly called East Pakistan and once part of India, the West Bengalis have remained citizens of the Republic of India. Quite often they don't seem to have liked it much. They have manifested their disagreement with Delhi in the volatile fashion shared both by East and West Bengalis, but they have remained, despite it all, Indian.

It will be interesting to see whether and to what extent the Bengalis as a whole will now feel the development of their identity as a people becomes more powerful than the identity that pulled them apart, the Muslim East Bengalis' desire to form an Islamic society.

The creation of a Bangladeshi airline, though it is irrelevant to the requirements of most Bangladeshis, does fill an important symbolic purpose. New countries, however desperate their economic plight, put on the trappings of an identity in order to help in the development of some kind of national consciousness. That is why anthems, flags, national airlines and sometimes a steelworks and a dam or two, which are the national equivalent of optional extras like a sliding roof or air conditioning in a car, so often go together with a new name in the post-colonial situation.

Sometimes the problems of creating a meaningful national identity are almost overwhelming. This is often because the colony that the new country supersedes was carved out with no regard for tribal, cultural or even geographical factors, but merely as a political compromise between two major colonial powers who agreed to frontiers that looked approximately symmetrical on the map.

Both Nigeria, which hasn't changed its name, and Zaire, which has, are artificial creations and both have suffered agonies in their search for an identity. They were formed at conferences in Europe. Zaire, as the so-called Congo Free State, was taken as a private fief by the Belgian King Leopold II after a congress in Berlin in 1884. Nigeria's future was settled at another European conference after a series of nasty little incidents between Britain and France in the West African area 14 years later.

After years of misrule the Congo Free State eventually became the Belgian Congo. In 1960 the Belgians withdrew and the Congo became independent. Almost immediately the most violent civil war blew up, conducted partially on tribal lines but, it is now agreed, fostered by a number of outside interests. After some years it ended and the Congo has so far, despite various further rumblings, to its own and everyone else's astonishment, remained in one piece.

It is hardly surprising that the present head of state spends much of his time and energy endeavouring to propagate a feeling of national consciousness. To begin with, the country's name was confusing: there was another Congo, a former French colony. In order to distinguish them one was called Congo (Brazzaville) and the other Congo (Kinshasa). Congo (Kinshasa) soon changed its name again and became Zaire.

In Zaire the names of the major cities were changed: Leopoldville has become Kinshasa, Stanleyville is Kisangani, and Elisabethville is Lubumbashi. Even the first and surnames of people have been or are being, if you'll pardon the expression, Zairicised.

This is an extract from an article in *The Guardian* of 12 May 1977:

'It was no surprise to see a poster at a recent Kinshasa rally reading "Zaire is neither to the right, nor to the left, nor of the centre".

'Zaire is Mobutu, who changed the name of his country just as he changed his own in 1971.

'Joseph Desire Mobutu and the Congo Republic were Africanised, as was every Christian name in the country in the interests of an African identity. Within this concept the President has harnessed twentieth century media techniques to promote what is translated as "Mobutism" — the ancient image of a powerful chief who rules through fear and favour in a kingdom that stretches far beyond the narrow confines of ethnic geography.

'This policy is less a measure of the President's enormous vanity than an expression of his conviction that the centrifugal forces which produced such bloody unrest in the old Congo can only be contained by the symbolism rather than the substance of power centralised in one supreme leader.

'This explains the extraordinary range of symbols with which Zaire's leader has surrounded himself, including the nightly colour television presentation of the President as a god-like figure swooping from the clouds!'

Zaire is a big and important country in African terms. It is making a powerful, consistent and probably quite thorough effort to create a national identity and to manifest this identity internationally.

Nigeria's identity problems are quite as acute as Zaire's. Like Zaire, Nigeria was formed with a complete lack of respect for the racial, cultural and religious identities of its inhabitants. The legacy of this has been the Biafran civil war, a series of coups, military government, and a number of differing and so far temporary patterns of regional reorganisation. So diverse are the cultures and histories of the peoples of Nigeria and so acute are its problems of identity that it has proved virtually impossible to teach Nigerian history to school children. In many schools English history is taught instead. Quite what effect this has on the development of a Nigerian identity is perhaps best not explored too closely.

Many African countries that are smaller and less important to the rest of the world have also changed their names. All have done it for the same reasons: they wanted to create a feeling of identity, of pride, of unity, and of cohesiveness internally among peoples who for one reason or another had not felt this previously, and they wanted to let the outside world know that they were something and somebody. As we shall see later in this book, to carry out a corporate identity programme for a business operating in a sophisticated climate with modern communication technology is very difficult and rarely succeeds completely, but to do the same thing in a small African state with very little money and not much in the way of technology is infinitely harder.

A measure of the success or failure that some of the smaller African states have achieved can perhaps be given by trying to match up a list of new names of African states with their former ones.

Here is a list of new names:
Botswana
Lesotho
Zambia
Malawi
Mali
Burundi

Here are their previous names in a different order:
Ruanda Urundi
French Sudan
Nyasaland
Northern Rhodesia
Basutoland
Bechuanaland

It is a sad reflection both of our interest in and knowledge of Africa and of the failure of the African nations' identity programmes that so few of us can match the one list against the other entirely accurately (they are actually in reverse order).

Some new countries, however, have had no trouble in making it clear who and what they are. Israel is one of the countries that has emerged within the last 30 years with a powerful, idiosyncratic and relevant corporate identity.

The Israelis have not only created a state, a flag, an anthem, an airline, an army and tourist resorts, but they have also developed a weapons industry, a brand of oranges (Jaffa), a new language (modern Hebrew is not biblical Hebrew) and virtually a brand new people. The Sabras—native Israelis—have little in common with Jews of the Diaspora. In fact many Israelis, and particularly the more recent arrivals, who have little in common with one another except that they call themselves or are called Jews, need to undergo a powerful course of indoctrination in order to appreciate that they are members of a very different society from the one they have just left.

The Israelis take care of this by making new Israelis learn Hebrew and, if young enough, join the army— preferably at the same time. The Israelis also make liberal use of such meagre traditional visual symbolism as is available: the seven-branched candlestick and the star of David are predominant features of many modern Israeli artefacts, particularly those sold to tourists.

Israel's problems are particularly complex. On the one hand, Jewish tradition and lore is real and complex; it strikes familiar chords in the hearts of Jews who have been brought up more or less traditionally. On the other hand, much Jewish tradition is connected with religious rites and practices that have little or no place in a modern democratic society. Indeed, some religious Jews refuse to recognise the State of Israel although they actually live in it.

Clearly the conflict between a modern democratic society and an ancient religion forms at least part of the conflict between the identities of Jews as Jews and Jews as Israelis. The problems which the Israeli state has in connection with inter-marriage, bizarre in a twentieth-century society, relate to this conflict of identities.

Jews living outside Israel have an identity that doesn't necessarily have a lot to do with religion either. It probably derives from the ghetto, at least in part. Jewish humour is a very powerful component of this identity, but Jewish humour doesn't always go down very well in Israel. Does General Moshe Dayan think that *Portnoy's Complaint* is funny? Probably not.

What seems to be happening is that the Israeli identity is getting less and less like the Jewish identity—which is a strange thing because Israel was formed so that Jews could have a home of their own to go to and feel at home in.

Countries with larger and more secure histories than those with which we have just been dealing tend to take their national identity much more for granted. Characteristics that have become ingrained over generations are not usually buffed-up, polished and consciously manipulated unless some major political change takes place. Quite often though, an attempt is made to change the way a people behaves. Within the past generation the Chinese, the Cubans, the South Vietnamese and the Cambodians have all had their societies reshaped.

It's difficult to know to what extent this really changes a people. Does the new government simply emphasise different facets of a personality that was there already, or does it inculcate entirely new characteristics?

Somehow the identity of a country with a long and relatively secure background seems to remain stable over a long period, although obviously the way it is governed can seem to change or modify its identity from time to time.

Russia is an interesting example of this. It has had the most dramatic changes in government, but it still has a consistency in style and purpose, and a continuity from the days of the Czars. Many of its institutions have remained the same, or at least very similar, even though their names have changed.

The KGB, the secret police, fulfils the same roles as did the Czarist Checka. Characteristics we can recognise from Chekov are still apparent. Uniforms still proliferate amongst servants of the state. The names of many of its cities have changed, but even this isn't a Soviet characteristic—it was Czar Nicholas II who changed St Petersburg to Petrograd, which of course then became Leningrad in 1924. In terms of literary progression there is a clear line between the great nineteenth-century writers—Dostoevski, Tolstoi and Chekov—and the Soviet masters, Pasternak and Solzhenitsyn, even in their sometimes ambivalent or hostile attitude to the current regime.

Some people would say that Russia's political aims and intentions have not altered since the days of the Romanoffs either, and that even the manner in which the country conducts its external affairs has continuity.

Of course the major change in terms of visual symbolism since 1917 is that the double-headed Romanoff eagle has been replaced by the hammer and sickle and the Red Flag. The hammer and sickle are not Russia's alone, however, and have, together with the clenched fist, been generously shared with many other countries professing Soviet-style socialism.

The hammer and sickle don't have the same simplicity and strength as many other visual symbols of faith. In graphic design terms they come well down the list. It is only consistent repetition that makes them seem to work at all.

Visually, for the most part Russia has followed a traditional pattern since the Revolution. Russian dolls still look like Russian dolls did before 1917. Russian soldiers and sailors still dress in a recognisably traditional way.

We can, however, detect certain post-revolutionary facets of visual identity—a style that is not so much traditional Russian as Communist Russian. Architecture, for example, has changed sharply: the wedding cake architecture so favoured by Russian architects of the 1930s and 1950s is particularly Russian and it seems to have no pre-revolutionary counterpart.

The Russian language has also changed quite considerably in some ways. This must account, at least in part, for the curious names and appearance of Russian and other East European exporting and importing organisations—Sovexport, Bulgarimport, Machinex, Medimpex, Pharmexpo (I'm not even sure how many of these are real and how many I've invented). At another

TYAZHPROMEXPORT

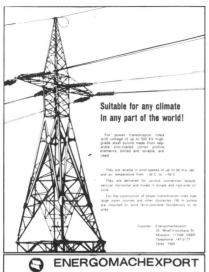

TECHMASHEXPORT

ATOMENERGOEXPORT

level, Russian consumer goods packaging projects a very clear aspect of the country's corporate identity and is particularly idiosyncratic and characteristic.

Genuine Russian Vodka MOSKOVSKAYA brand is 'distilled and bottled in the USSR for SOJUZPLODO-IMPORT' (say it Sod-you-plod-o-import) 'MOSCOW'. I haven't made that up, it says so on the label. Foreign imitators are, of course, called Borzoi, Smirnoff, Romanoff, Russian Imperial, Cossack, Vladivar and, for all I know, Ivan the Terrible, but you can always tell the real thing because it looks so artificial and strikingly unattractive.

What characterises the Russian identity and that of its East European neighbours in packaging and advertising is its drab, unimaginative appearance, its lack of any grace,

Genuine Russian vodka (top) and its genuine Western imitators

TIMOTHY QUALLINGTON

its clumsy pointlessness and its poor technical quality. All of this of course derives from the fact that the reality of Russian life does not call for sophisticated advertising and the other expensive technology that highly skilled marketing demands. That's why our vodka labels look more attractive, although their stuff may well taste better.

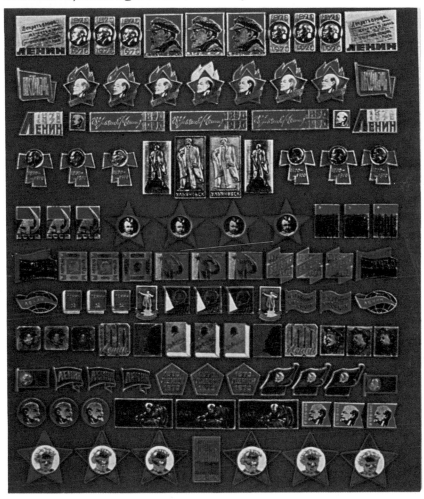

Red symbolism

Chapter 4
The personality of the modern industrial corporation
Is corporate planning the last refuge of the romantic?
The international style and regionalism.

The modern corporation operates on the implicit assumption that it can control its own destiny. All the elaborate apparatus of corporate planning, with the modish management consultancy techniques that come in one year and go out the next, are sold to big companies by their hand-maidens, the management consultancies, on the tacit understanding that if enough of these systems are injected into the organisation it will behave in a well organised, sensible, logical, efficient and rational manner. The belief is that by so doing the corporation will be able to influence outside circumstances and situations sufficiently to continue to grow, or at worst to ensure its own survival.

There is only one thing wrong with this principle. It ignores the fact that the world is in more or less constant turmoil; that many people, including some of those in important political positions, behave irrationally in their public as well as in their private lives; and that the nature of human society is that it should operate in chaos.

Terence Griffin, the creative consultant, describes corporate planning as in some senses the last refuge of the romantic. He thinks that in the minds of some planners there is a kind of lunatic belief that they can control the world.

How many of the thousands of companies all over the world who were doing their corporate planning in the late 1960s took into account the Yom Kippur war, the oil crisis and all the resulting developments? Apparently none, not even the oil companies themselves.

There is something ingenuous, even a little simple-minded, in the idea that it is possible for one company battling against the chaos of the whole world to plan its own future, and yet this is the basis on which most major and many smaller companies work. No wonder that the corporate planning process has what are described as 'malfunctions' from time to time.

On the other hand, the corporation has no alternative to planning. Decisions involving the expenditure of vast sums of money, decisions to invest in a new type of aircraft or a new steel mill, to buy or sell a paint company, cannot be taken on a whim; they have to be taken in the light of the most accurate information available. Many decisions are of the either/or type—'We put money into either India or

45

Denmark', say—but usually they are much more complicated than this. They involve making decisions about the future growth rate of nations, their likely political developments, the extent to which trade unions will be co-operative, the manner in which the market for the product will develop, what competitors might do, how rates of exchange will vary, how potential customers will react, and a whole series of more detailed questions deriving from these. It would be impossible for the modern industrial or commercial enterprise to go about its business if it did not plan.

But planning often goes badly wrong if it doesn't have an intuitive element, or if this intuitive element fails. The Ford Motor Company, which must have one of the most skilful and, on balance, most successful planning operations in the world, once had a huge investment in France. It owned a chunk of the Simca company, currently Chrysler's only successful European operation. Ford got out of Simca in the 1950s because it didn't believe in France's future. Since the middle 1960s it has been struggling to get back into France again.

The corporation cannot resolve the paradox that, on the one hand, planning does not really work properly because people are irrational and unpredictable and the world operates haphazardly, while on the other hand it must have some basis on which to take investment and marketing decisions. So it has to plan, however unreliably.

But a plan, however tentative, somehow develops a life of its own when it gets put on paper. It becomes more certain, more comfortingly reliable. It encourages the company into feeling that everything is under control and all buttoned up. It wouldn't do to let on that the whole apparatus of planning is an elaborate, inefficient and unreliable aid to common sense and that things go wrong more often than not. On the contrary, it seems to be important to cultivate the opposite impression—that the organisation is a quiet powerhouse run by some kind of benign super-intelligence who knows when to launch new products, when to withdraw old ones and when to lay down new plants, who can accurately predict stock market trends and performances, and who unfailingly understands the mind of the consumer.

This myth explains why so many companies look the way they do to outsiders. They need to look bland, smooth and unwrinkled, all-knowing, all-seeing, in order to make it clear that they can create order out of chaos, even when they know—and we know—that they cannot.

All major companies are in the same boat. Whether they come from Germany, Sweden, Italy or the USA, they all need to look as though they know it all, as though whatever it is that's happening, they've planned for it.

Of course, there are exceptions to this general rule. If the corporation is the direct result of one man's dream, like the Disney Corporation, it isn't going to look much like a mainstream big corporation. It's companies like, say, Siemens of Germany, with fingers in a lot of pies, that try to look as though they know it all.

If companies share the idea of corporate omniscience, it is also inevitable that they will tend to look similar. To allow humour or whimsy to play a part in the way they look or behave would be to imply that the company had human as opposed to superhuman characteristics, that it could laugh, cry, lose its temper, make mistakes, forget things or even go mad.

Since the intention of the corporation is to look superhuman and not human it is inevitable that its visual style will tend to be severe, powerful and withdrawn. The corporation will look classical rather than romantic; cubist rather than surrealist.

There are some other factors that influence the way companies look and behave. Until after World War Two there were relatively few companies operating on a truly world-wide basis. The major oil companies, the big US motor manufacturers and a few others like Unilever were running what we would now call multinational enterprises, but most really big companies kept within carefully organised and regulated spheres of influence. Trade associations and cartels of one kind or another parcelled out the world conveniently. The process was made easier because many of the major manufacturing countries had well defined markets.

Before World War Two the Americans had the US, Latin America and the Philippines; the British had their empire; the French, Dutch, Italians and Belgians theirs; Germany dominated many of the central European markets, but of course had no truly captive markets—a situation it subsequently tried to redress; and Japan, although a much smaller force industrially than today, was also attempting vigorously to expand its sphere of influence —hence the Greater Asia Co-Prosperity Sphere, which was the name Japan used to describe its transient wartime conquests.

For most practical purposes these big protected markets enabled manufacturers to retain their national idiosyncracies. Only the Germans and the Japanese understood what it was like to market products in an alien environment. Perhaps their post-war success in international trade indicates that they learnt something from this experience.

After World War Two this situation changed: empires disappeared, new trading communities formed, tariff

Regional British bus service liveries (above) compared with their National Bus Company successor (see page 50)

barriers were reduced, cartels were no longer so fashionable and, above all, communication in physical terms became much easier. Global marketing was in.

Within the past few years companies with pretensions to real size, even those in the second or third league, have had to operate all over the world. In the 1930s a firm such as Poclain, the French earth moving equipment company with an annual turnover according to *The Economist* of 22 January 1977 of about 400 million US dollars, would probably have operated in metropolitan France, some of the French North and West African colonies, and in Indo China and the French mandated territories of Syria and Lebanon. Before 1939 Poclain, even if it had then been relatively as large as it is today, would have operated within a cultural environment that was French. Today it operates in a wholly international cultural framework. Poclain has a plant at Fredericksburg, Virginia, USA and operates all over the Common Market, in Eastern Europe, in many countries of the Far East and in South America.

This means that Poclain, if it is to be intelligible to its markets, has got to be less French than it would have been before World War Two. It's got to look less French and behave and think in a less French way. (Since it has joined the US group Tenneco this problem no longer exists.)

Equally, JCB, a British company operating in a similar field, has the same problem. JCB is not a large company in world terms; it isn't that big even in British terms. Before 1939 the chances are that JCB would have operated solely within the British Imperial networks; today its marketing operations are international.

JCB, if it is to sell in the United States, must be intelligible to Americans. It has to adopt a style that is internationally acceptable. The development of global marketing is a very powerful homogenising force, even for smaller companies such as Poclain and JCB.

Badische Anilin- & Soda-Fabrik of Ludwigshafen is a highly successful and huge international chemical company. It was once familiarly known as Badische, but non-German speakers find Badische difficult to read and to say. Badische Anilin- & Soda-Fabrik needs to look competitive with British ICI, with American Dupont and with Dutch Akzo everywhere in the world. It has to look and feel comfortable in places as culturally diverse as New Zealand, Finland and Colombia, so Badische Anilin- & Soda-Fabrik calls itself BASF, which anyone can pronounce, and it dresses itself in an internationally acceptable style.

In international marketing it is inevitable that the

lowest common denominator will prevail. For the sake of ubiquity all companies, whatever their national origins, look more and more like each other. If we take some chemical companies we can see this very clearly.

In some industries, particularly those with most international affiliations, this development has gone much further than in others. The aircraft industry, for example, which is American dominated, speaks American. Even such staunch nationalists as the French find it difficult to resist this pattern, simply because American influence throughout the industry is so strong.

Furniture manufacturing, on the other hand, which is still largely a craft industry, has firm national roots. Danish furniture and Italian furniture look very different and to a considerable extent are marketed on the basis of genuine differences.

Some furniture still reflects the character of the country it comes from— Danish (left) and Italian (above) seating

As the world continues to shrink and people all over the world develop similar tastes in what they wear, how they spend their money and what they want, the big corporation with its so-called international design style will become more of a force for homogenisation.

And while the movement that makes everything bigger and encourages people to behave in a similar and predictable way constantly increases in momentum and force, there is another almost equally powerful movement headed in a precisely contrary direction. This is a tide running in the direction of keeping things local, keeping things simple and making things smaller. This trend is not new or even recent, even though it has currently become more fashionable.

In fact, another manifestation of the movement—regionalism—has a very long history indeed. The Bretons, Alsatians and Corsicans in France, the Basques and Catalans in Spain, and the Scots and Welsh in Britain have all been campaigning for years for some kind of regional autonomy. In recent years, however, their activities have become considerably more visible. And as if this isn't sufficient, the Walloons and Flemings in Belgium and the French-speaking Canadians are also manifesting their belief that local loyalties, habits and customs are in many respects more significant and meaningful than larger, more remote ones.

For the most part this feeling has been neglected or ignored by world-wide organisations, especially in terms of the way they project themselves visually.

Until a few years ago the regional bus services in Britain had a charming diversity in colour, style and name that emphasised their local character. Colin Forbes has pointed out that the design scheme for the National Bus Company, the successor to the old regional companies, which he and many other eminent designers happen to regard as very poor, also misses the opportunity to retain some of the regional character of the bus services.

People don't like it when their roots are torn up and thrown away in the interest of some central homogenising force for neatness. There is no doubt a good reason to harmonise all road signs so that they look the same and convey standard information, even though in doing this we lose the characteristic feeling of place and locality that was so strong and attractive, but it is difficult to justify the destruction of the regional bus and coach liveries that meant so much to many local people.

Some years ago when I was involved in discussions

with the Gas Council, as it then was, on the identity of Gas in Britain, the arguments which the regional Gas Boards put up to defend their own identities on the grounds of local associations were, in fact, very strong, although it is arguable whether the Gas Boards were really small enough to sustain that line of discussion, and in the event under a different hand they do look like one large unit.

There can be no doubt at all that, as concepts like devolution and regionalism become more fashionable all over the world, corporate identity programmes must take this into account. There is no technical reason why this should not be done.

There are a few cases in which regional factors are taken into account. The British Airports Authority is a nationalised industry that looks after many of the major and some of the smaller airports in Britain. The reality of the BAA is at the airports.

The old national BAA identity and (bottom) its new decentralised airport successor

Each airport has a different problem. Each airport creates its own loyalties and the passengers who need to deal with airport employees are not interested in the BAA, only in whether they work for the individual airport. This was a classic case for a decentralised identity.

For the most part though, the modern industrial corporation has been caught on the wrong foot by regionalism and by most of the implications of presenting itself on a modest and human scale. This is not surprising in view of other aspects of the company's imagery. What it says is often as important as what it looks like. I have had many discussions with chairmen and chief executives about the problems discussed in this book. Almost without exception when we have had our initial meetings I have been subjected to what I now think of as the 'forward, onward, upward and into the future' speech—'the company is moving forward, we are having some temporary difficulties, but the general trends are favourable, etc, etc'— even when it was clear to me, to my hosts and to the world at large that the company was about to fall flat on its face.

It is hardly surprising in view of all this that one superhuman company looks much the same as another. Would it be too much to suggest that the vision most companies try to project is that of Voltaire's Dr Pangloss— that 'all is for the best in this, the best of possible worlds'?

Chapter 5
What happens when companies merge
The story of VFW and Fokker, and some less detailed examples.

In one merger after another nowadays the same mistakes are made. Time after time companies make the most complex arrangements to merge their interests. They enter into elaborate financial agreements, they claim that the companies involved in the merger are complementary, that two plus two will this time really equal five—and yet time after time it doesn't happen. They present themselves in a confused and confusing manner that almost always emphasises that they don't seem to know where they are and why they are merging. A classic example is the case of VFW and Fokker.

In 1946 the German aircraft industry was in ruins. Its factories had been destroyed and its best technicians were either in jail or had moved abroad. Its highly sophisticated wartime products were the subject of close study by the engineers of its former enemies; later both Russian and American space programmes were based to some extent on German technology. There seemed little prospect for German genius to re-emerge in this branch of engineering.

Gradually, however, the aircraft factories started up again. Some of them, like Messerschmitt and Heinkel, began by building tiny economy cars—bubble cars as they were called. Others made very light aircraft or carried out repair and maintenance work for the allied air forces.

Slowly, as Germany began to take up military commitments again, its aircraft industry started to build under licence, and although the industry did not grow to its former size it eventually became quite large. It is now the third largest of the aircraft industries in Europe with about 40,000 employees.

During the late 1950s and early 1960s aircraft companies were merging all over Europe. There were two reasons for this: first, individual airframe makers simply couldn't afford to develop the sophisticated aircraft that were by then required; and second, European makers had no chance to compete with the American industry with its much larger domestic market unless the companies coalesced into fewer, larger units.

So more or less simultaneously in Britain, France and Germany most of the smaller factories were pushed into a few big groups. In Britain, the British Aircraft Corporation and Hawker Siddeley were formed. In Germany, two units were also created, Messerschmitt-Bölkow-Blohm—usually known as MBB—based in Munich, and another slightly larger company based in Bremen.

The new group based in Bremen was made up of a few largish independent companies—Focke-Wulf, Weserflug and ERNO—and a number of smaller ones—Heinkel, the aircraft bits of the locomotive and lorry builders Henschel, the light aircraft companies Sportavia Putzer, Rheinflugzeugbau and some others. Almost all these companies had their own research and development teams, their own, mostly illusory, plans for expansion, their own traditional activities of light aircraft, space research, licensed manufacture, and of course a natural pride in their achievements and history.

But the merger would have made no sense if each of the units had been allowed to carry on exactly as before. Its whole point was to build one large unit, and that meant breaking up the smaller ones.

While some of the decisions involved were entirely practical—how many units should continue to exist, where could research and development effort best be deployed, for example—many of the decisions were also emotional.

One of the key emotional issues was what the organisation should be called. The largest, best known and most prestigious of the companies was Focke-Wulf. But to call the group Focke-Wulf would be to emphasise the significance of one company over all the others.

A second, almost equally important, question was what the group's products should be called. The organisation made aircraft and a variety of other products, from touring caravans used as summer holiday homes at one end of the scale, to sophisticated hardware and software for the European space programme at the other.

Even within the aircraft field there were problems. The main product was an airliner under development by Focke-Wulf. Should this be called by an entirely new and unknown name or should it capitalise on the better known names that formed part of the group—Focke-Wulf or even Heinkel?

It was decided to call the new group Vereinigte Flugtechnische Werke, which means United Aircraft Works. Non-Germans could not pronounce the name, so it was shortened to VFW, which incidentally some of its American contacts thought meant Veterans of Foreign Wars. Some of its products were called VFW, but others, perhaps less important or run by parts of the group with an obstinate and independent streak, kept their existing names.

Almost inevitably the compromise maintained the confusion. ERNO remained ERNO, although it admitted to a tenuous connection with VFW. Sportavia Putzer remained Sportavia Putzer, and so did Rheinflugzeugbau, though they too made formal gestures of obeisance in the direction of VFW. A vertical take off (VTOL) military aircraft designed to compete with Hawker Siddeley's Harrier remained puzzlingly anonymous as VAK 191B, which could even have been confused with the Russian YAK. The main new project, the new civil airliner, was called VFW 614.

Gradually the companies comprising VFW settled down uneasily together. Gradually too, both inside the company and outside, VFW began to develop some kind of shadowy identity, although this was related almost entirely to the 614 commercial aircraft project.

In real terms there was not a lot of co-operation between the various parts of VFW; the independent units tried to keep as far away from each other as possible. Although some attempts were made to promote the corporate name, the individual company names were and remained better known at many levels than the group name.

For the most part the people inside VFW still thought of themselves as Heinkel or Focke-Wulf, ERNO or Weserflug. For most of them, except at the highest levels, VFW had no real meaning. Outsiders, even informed ones, had very little idea about what VFW made or how big it was—they couldn't describe the idea of VFW.

And then came the next merger. The Dutch aircraft company called Fokker had nothing to do either with Focke-Wulf or with the German aircraft industry. It was founded by Anton Fokker, a pioneer Dutch aviator who built aircraft in Germany under the Fokker name in the 1914 war. One of these aircraft, the Fokker triplane, gained fame as the favourite machine of the Red Baron, von Richthofen, and his successor, Hermann Goering.

When the First World War was over, Anton Fokker smuggled much of his equipment out of Germany into his homeland and set up another Fokker company. This was a totally different affair; Fokker's main product between the wars was a triple-engined civil airliner. So while the first Fokker company was German, glamorous, romantic and noted for its warplanes, the second was Dutch, staid, reliable and noted for its civil airliners.

Fokker's great days came after World War Two, when it designed, built and sold the F27 or Friendship, one of the most successful civil aircraft ever to emerge from Europe. Fokker then developed and introduced the much bigger F28, which in sales terms started off very slowly. This hurt the company and Fokker realised that it too could no longer live alone. Like the other middle-sized European aircraft companies it had to merge. It turned to VFW.

Like so many other mergers, the merger of Fokker and VFW, which took place in 1970, looked extremely attractive on paper. Fokker had a first-class marketing and sales organisation, a history of sound, practical aircraft manufacturing and an excellent, clear image. VFW had brilliant, unconventional engineering, a very widespread of products, no real commercial know-how, virtually no image at all, and the implicit backing of Germany, Europe's richest state.

In fact, no two organisations were more different from each other in tradition, business style and research and development activity. Fokker was a tight, practical, pragmatic company with a clear attitude based on a generation of tough and highly successful experience in aircraft manufacturing and selling. VFW was a confederation of different companies that had existed on a bizarre mixture of mundane contracts and far-out research and development work. It had vast ambitions, not much organisation, and virtually no practical experience. As if all this was not enough, Fokker was Dutch and VFW was German.

A great deal of thought was given to the organisation of the new company. What made life particularly difficult was that there was not then, nor is there yet, any possibility of setting up a European community company because the European Economic Community has as yet no laws permitting such an arrangement. So much, perhaps, for federation in practice.

It is difficult to believe that much time was invested in working out the psychological effects of the merger on the people working in the companies. Nor is it likely that the implications of the merger on the group's suppliers, customers, potential customers and other outsiders were fully considered.

In identity terms the problems were, first, did the new organisation need a new name, neither Fokker nor VFW? Or should it be called either Fokker or VFW? Or should it be called Fokker-VFW or VFW-Fokker? Second, what should its products be called? Should they continue to use their existing names, should they all get new names, or should some other course be adopted? Would it be desirable, for instance, to call all civil aircraft by one name, all military aircraft by another and all space activities by a third? Third, if a new system was to be developed, how far should all this penetrate the organisation? Should all purchasing be carried out under one name, say the corporate name, which might make the advantages of size manifest, or alternatively, would it be better to keep the existing name structure for purchasing purposes?

In the event nothing much was done. The holding company was called Zentralgesellschaft VFW-Fokker. Its head office was located in Düsseldorf, approximately half-way between the two main factories at Amsterdam and Bremen. The German half of the company was called VFW-Fokker and the Dutch half Fokker-VFW.

The Dutch half of the company continued to call its products Fokker F27 and F28, and it continued to use Fokker signs all over its factories, vehicles and sales literature. In fact, it would not be too much to say that so far as possible the Dutch acted as though the merger had not taken place.

In Bremen the situation was rather more confused. VFW was well aware that Fokker was a better known name than its own and so it attached the word Fokker to VFW when and where it thought this might be useful. On the other hand, the VFW companies that had formerly pursued an independent line continued to do so. ERNO remained ERNO, for example, and Sportavia Putzer remained Sportavia Putzer. The VFW 614, although built by the VFW-Fokker organisation in Bremen and theoretically marketed by Fokker-VFW International in Amsterdam, continued to be known as the VFW 614. This led to a series of complications and absurdities such as that shown in the advertisement illustrated here.

Both VFW-Fokker (that is, Bremen) and Fokker-VFW (that is, Amsterdam) were partners on the Airbus programme. They were shown in illustrations and described in literature as separate companies—the one, believe it or not, described as VFW-Fokker and the other as Fokker-VFW.

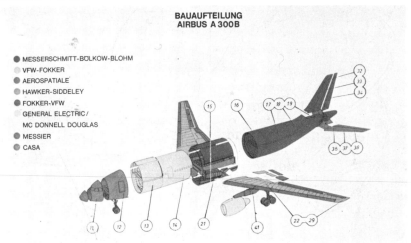

If insiders were confused, outsiders such as suppliers and journalists were completely bemused by it all. Quite respectable and well informed journalists failed to comprehend what the relationship between the companies was. Even some suppliers dealing with different parts of the group at the same time were not clear about the extent to which they were related, or indeed whether they were related at all.

The merger didn't lead to greater strength; it led, at least for a time, to greater weakness, to diffusion of effort, and to squabbling and to jostling for position. It is difficult to tell how much this lack of clarity cost the organisation. There are two factors to consider here, internal and external. First there is the internal bickering, the maintenance of loyalties, traditions and systems entirely inappropriate to a new situation, which sometimes goes so far as the retention of competitive research and development departments and even competition in selling. And then there is the confusion so far as the outside world is concerned, which results in people dealing with the organisation being unclear about how big it is and even what it does.

When the merger was being planned, those responsible did not sufficiently consider emotions—they ignored what goes on in people's minds. They didn't think that loyalties, traditions and attitudes and the way these manifested themselves in names, signs and colours were sufficiently important. Nor did they consider them to be of commercial importance or, if they did, they thought that these were problems that would somehow look after themselves.

When a merger takes place so much attention is paid to getting the financial part of the equation right that there hardly seems to be enough energy left to deal with all the other aspects.

VFW-Fokker is only one example, perhaps a rather more complex and extreme one than most, of how a company must take its identity into account when it changes and develops.

What should the VFW-Fokker organisation have done? The new organisation had a complex and difficult problem that needed sophisticated outside professional help. The company could not solve its own problems because there were too many emotions and susceptibilities involved that would almost inevitably have clouded the judgement of those concerned.

In fact, VFW-Fokker recognised its problems, or at least some people in the company did, and outside consultants were called in. The consultants pointed out the existing confusion and explained what the company was losing by perpetuating the existing situation. They then made three linked proposals.

The first was that the group name should be changed. The second was that the company should go through its store of well-known names and select some to brand the different activities clearly. The third was that this should be linked with a new visual identity applied to the visual manifestations of the group.

What this would have meant in practice was that a new group name would have been launched. The consultants emphasised that it was important for the name to be neither Fokker nor VFW so that neither side could be seen to have won.

Let us say the name was Aerospace of Europe, which it was not. Everybody would have been employed by this company. No more ERNO or Fokker or VFW; they would all have gone.

So after a time there would have been no more arguments about the Fokker way of doing things or the Weserflug way, or for that matter about the Dutch way of doing things compared with the German way. All standards of manufacture and design and purchasing would have been the same.

In every activity except one Aerospace of Europe would have replaced all the old names and therefore eventually the old ideologies, emotions, frictions and jealousies. The one level at which it was recommended to keep other names was for the customer. VFW-Fokker was the repository of once well known, greatly respected and in some cases much feared names. The suggestion made by the consultants was that, in order to identify the various separate activities of the company and in order to make clear the size, scope and wealth of expertise within it, some—the best—of the traditional names within the group should be used to describe certain parts of it.

Since Fokker had a reputation in medium-sized civil aircraft, all machines of this type produced by the group were to have been called Fokker, irrespective of whether they were designed and built at Amsterdam or Bremen. There would therefore have been a family of three aircraft, Fokker F27, Fokker F28 and the newly named Fokker F29 —formerly VFW 614—all marketed through the Fokker Civil Aircraft Division of Aerospace of Europe.

On the military side the name Heinkel would perhaps have been suitable. So that instead of VFW's VAK 191B vertical take off aircraft, Aerospace of Europe would have had its Heinkel VTOL, a name with somewhat greater punch. The branding system would have been extended over the entire company, covering all its activities.

The third recommendation was that all of this needed to be held together with a visual system. The visual system—which in a very simple form is a house style, some colours, some type and a symbol—would in the case of VFW-Fokker have needed to be both complex and flexible.

What was required was a system in which there was opportunity for the corporate name to be more important than the brands or for the brands to be more significant than the corporation, as appropriate. The visual system needed to allow each brand to present itself powerfully, but to be clearly seen as part of the overall corporate structure. It had to work effectively and with appropriate modulations of tone whenever it appeared. It involved the use of the whole of the design consultant's graphic paraphernalia.

The suggestions that were made to VFW-Fokker were in fact classic corporate identity proposals devised to deal with a classic corporate identity problem.

VFW-Fokker hovered indecisively. Yes, perhaps a single group name would be advantageous, but why couldn't it be Fokker or VFW? Everything that was proposed had disadvantages and drawbacks as well as advantages. These were debated and the political lines were drawn. The Fokker people, seeing a clear attempt to restrict their autonomy, resisted, while the VFW people, anxious to compromise and be good partners, were not too sure what to do. In the event nothing happened, opportunities were missed and everything went on as before. If the decision had been about a more tangible resource—capital equipment, a new project, even people— it would never have been treated in this way.

But in some strange way finance, management technology, corporate strategy and getting all the sums right are regarded as a kind of commercial 'machismo' while all the rest of it, the way human beings feel, the way the company changes and develops as a result of a merger or a takeover, is thought of as sissy, as not important, as not 'men's work'.

In fact, the cost to a company of leaving this detritus— this carnage of brand names, company names, outdated outward symbols and imagery, of not studying the problem and not doing the job properly—is incalculable. Internally the confusions and jealousies, the doubling up of work, the suspicions, the witholding of vital sales or technical information all cost enormous sums of money. And externally, if the job is not seen to have been done, if the new reality is not made clear, people will simply assume that nothing has changed, either for better or worse.

The simple truth is that putting companies together on paper is not the same as putting them together in reality. It demands the creation of a common culture. It means that when employees visit one another's factories and offices they find familiar things, familiar names, familiar signs, familiar systems, even familiar furniture—things that make them feel at home. When this does not happen the relationships between merged units are strained and the benefits just do not emerge.

Perhaps even more significant as a cause for the confusion is that in a merger many companies do not understand how to use the various names that often seem to be scattered about so profusely.

On the one hand the merger is designed to create clarity, harmony and, above all, synergy. So it is vital to get everyone in the new group working together for the benefit of the group as a whole and not just for one part of it. It is vital to take advantage of economies in bulk purchasing, and to project the totality of the organisation to Wall Street, the City of London, potential customers, competitors and other interested groups, and this seems to mean the development of one consistent image. All of this appears to point towards one corporate name throughout the organisation.

On the other hand, however, the merged company almost inevitably consists of a group of organisations, each with its own loyal customers, long traditions, goodwill amongst the local community and its own employees, and it sometimes appears wantonly destructive to get rid of these in the interests of some kind of abstract unquantifiable advantage. This then points towards the continued use of a multiplicity of names.

Furthermore, there are usually powerful groups of people in any organisation whose particular interest it is to maintain the status quo. In personal terms the chief executive of an apparently independent organisation seems to have more status than the manager of a division in a group. The Managing Director of Sharp and Pointed Ltd, steel stockholders, founded in 1893, arriving in his Jaguar at the golf club on Sunday morning gets more respect than the Divisional Manager of the steel stockholding division of The International Bashitt and Benditt Corporation. Pressures from customers also play a large part in maintaining a complex naming structure.

So what with pressures from outside as well as those from within, it needs a very determined and strong-minded management to make the dramatic changes sometimes required when a merger takes place.

Patterns vary from industry to industry. The major British banks, which are so conservative and cautious in many ways, are highly experienced, realistic and very bold when it comes to mergers. This should come as no surprise because they all grew cannibalistically. When two banks merge, the smaller one generally sinks without trace.

The case of the so-called merger between Barclays and Martins which took place in Britain in 1968 is fairly typical. Both Barclays and Martins had been built up through takeover. Each had managed to retain its own name and eradicate those of its partners over the years. When Barclays merged with Martins exactly the same pattern was repeated.

A financial journalist described the merger as that of the anaconda and the rabbit. Within a few months Barclays had gobbled up Martins and today Martins Bank is hardly even a memory.

Although Barclays and Martins were both British banks they didn't have a great deal in common. Barclays was extremely big (2658 branches), Martins was relatively small (704 branches). Martins was in some senses and at least in some parts of the country rather an exclusive bank; its branches tended to be small, its architectural policy was advanced, and it cultivated a friendly, informal atmosphere. Barclays was big and bustling.

Clearly there was a lot of goodwill attached to the Martins name and many possibilities were open to Barclays. They could have run the two banks side by side or they could have had an up-market division called Martins, for example.

At the time of the merger there was a lot of talk that customers of Martins would resent the change and would leave in droves, but they failed to do so. It is true that at first a lot of Martins employees didn't like the idea of belonging to Barclays, but most of them had not wanted the merger anyway. The change in identity allowed them to understand their new position clearly: they were, for better or worse—but irrevocably—Barclays.

In almost every other industry such a merger would have started with some kind of compromise name like Barclay-Martin. There might have been some attempt to pretend that Martins was still independent. A sign-off might have been prepared—'Martins Bank, a member of the Barclays Group' would have appeared on stationery, advertisements and on all bank literature. The fascias on the two banks would have remained different and the illusion that Martins was still Martins and still independent might have been maintained.

Internally, rival departments would have been busily thwarting each other's activities and the multitudinous jealousies so common within large organisations would have been exacerbated. Rival marketing departments, building departments, advertising departments and personnel departments would have worked viciously but quietly against each other. Staff would have continued to refer to themselves as Martins or Barclays people. For some years Martins people would have retained an air of grievance, bitterly resenting their slow, inescapable and expensive decline. Barclays would have continued to resent and ultimately to ignore the increasingly irrelevant vapourings emerging from Martins.

Externally, former Martins customers would have complained about declining standards: 'It wasn't like this in the old days when Martins was Martins', they would have said, thereby constantly rubbing salt into the Martins wound. Martins would have gradually sunk into decline and eventually disappeared. It would have been a costly, agonising and entirely unnecessary operation. Happily, for the cost of a few bruises early on, everybody was spared agonies later.

Barclays was either clever or lucky; it totally obliterated the Martins identity. At the time of the merger Barclays introduced a design programme so that the old Barclays visual style, such as it was, disappeared at the same time as Martins.

Martins Bank, Gloucester Road, London— now Barclays Bank, Gloucester Road, London

Although they operated in totally different industries, the mergers between Barclays and Martins on the one hand, and VFW and Fokker on the other, had something in common. Both took place defensively. Barclays did not set out to acquire Martins—a merger between National Provincial and Westminster Bank set it off. Equally, Fokker and VFW only merged because each needed the extra size of the other in a world in which all the aircraft companies seemed to be getting together.

Both mergers were intended to create greater strength for a new single organisation rather than greater diversity of activity. In the case of Barclays this was single-mindedly remembered, whereas VFW-Fokker seemed to forget it somewhere along the way.

In both mergers there were a number of apparently complementary factors between the partners. Barclays was geographically strong in areas where Martins was weak; Fokker was strong in marketing where VFW was weak. While Barclays used their situation as an opportunity to make one name stronger, VFW and Fokker simply pussyfooted around. Barclays, having pursued the logic of the situation, emerged much stronger after a rather uncomfortable period. VFW-Fokker, having avoided the issue for a few years, has derived little benefit.

During the 1960s, when mergers were very fashionable and before small became beautiful, one merger took place after another. If two smaller companies were not very successful, the idea was that one larger one stuck together would somehow be better. Sometimes they were. More often, though, two not very successful smaller companies made one very much bigger not very successful company.

Why? Usually because they followed not the Barclays/Martins pattern but the VFW/Fokker pattern. The mergers were not really mergers at all. Nobody really mixed at any level. The potential economies of scale were not really seized. The duplicated marketing effort was not really halved. The product lines were not truly rationalised. The plethora of brand names, company names and corporate names was not really rationalised. The loyalties of staff and workers at all levels were not really harnessed to the new organisation. All that happened in practice was that yet another layer of management was added to an organisation already overloaded with management levels.

There are many reasons why this situation constantly recurs. Most are to do with a reluctance to grasp nettles. Here are two of them. First there is what is called 'goodwill', that is to say the financial value that is placed upon a reputation. With our current mania for attempting to quantify the unquantifiable we always attribute some kind of financial value to a name and, by implication, to the reputation behind it.

Like so many exercises of this kind, this works retrospectively. The values placed on the name relate not to its use in the present or the future, when it will appear in a new context, but to its past impact. The concept of goodwill is an attempt to introduce rational or quasi rational financial calculations into a situation that defies this kind of treatment. To take a hypothetical case, if British Leyland bought Rolls-Royce Motors and began to put Rolls-Royce radiators on Jaguars, within a short time the Rolls-Royce name would become virtually valueless.

We know this is true because Jaguar actually did this to Daimler. The Daimler name, once worth nearly as much as Rolls-Royce, is now false coin. A Daimler, as everyone knows, is a Jaguar wearing a top hat and spats.

Jaguar by Jaguar

Daimler by Jaguar

And what Rolls Royce would become if Jaguar got the chance

Oddly enough, Jaguar is now perpetrating the same treatment to Daimler that Daimler formerly gave out to Lanchester—plus ça change! This brings us to the second reason why names are retained and subjected, as Daimler has been, to the lingering death of a thousand cuts. Somehow people find it difficult to accept the obvious and are almost always reluctant to kill a name. This is particularly true in many so-called mergers in which the reality that one company has taken over another is fudged.

The retention of their name seems to be an inexpensive sop for the victors to throw to the vanquished. If the weaker party in a so-called merger emerges with nothing else, at least it can retain the appearance of equality in that both names appear on the letterhead. This particular kind of emotion—or rather emotionalism—reaches its peak in companies like the former English Electric Leo Marconi Computers—now part of ICL—in which all three parties to the merger insisted, for a time at least, on retaining their names, thereby rendering the new company name more or less unusable and completely incomprehensible.

In a merger a lot of difficult decisions have to be taken. In the end, when the intention is to create one organisation with one set of loyalties, to reduce overheads, research and development costs, selling costs, advertising costs, and really to make one effective unit out of two weaker ones, it does not help to pretend that nothing has happened.

In Germany the merger of the two ailing electrical giants AEG and Telefunken has produced the even sicker electrical mammoth called AEG-Telefunken.

In France the merger of the diverse electrical interests of Alsthom and the shipbuilding interests of Chantiers de L'Atlantique has created Alsthom-Atlantique.

Frankenstein's monster, although he was a bit on the mis-shapen side and had a few manufactured bits, at least had only one head. Many of today's industrial monsters have at least two.

The merger is, as many but apparently not enough organisations know, not a moment when things change by degrees but when they change in kind. It is the moment when a completely new set of loyalties is called for. If the leaders of African countries with their relatively limited experience of communication techniques understand this, it is strange that the world's industrial leaders cannot.

Chapter 6
The company and the community

What the community expects from the corporation.
How some companies react. Why corporations are bewildered.
'It is a sad reflection on the corporations
and the designers they have employed that, with a few exceptions,
the changes in society have passed them by.'

Every business organisation, however big or small, young or old, primitive or sophisticated, has social relationships. A sense of belonging emerges among its employees and is fostered institutionally. From the annual Christmas booze-up at which the contracts manager pours what he hopes is an aphrodisiac mixture of sparkling wine and vodka down the gullet of the girl from the typing pool, to the kind of cradle-to-the-grave security indulged in by the big, complex, old Japanese zaibatsu companies like Mitsui and Mitsubishi, the company foots the bill.

There is nothing new in the concept of social relationships within corporations. The British banks have had sporting and athletics clubs for generations. The 25-year watch presentation, the annual outing to the seaside and the Christmas party are all traditional, time-honoured manifestations of it.

The corporation has always had external relationships too. Even in the most extreme periods of laissez faire no company could do quite what it liked. The company has always had a relationship with the state.

Hours of employment were controlled, insurance schemes were introduced, factory inspectorates were established. This meant that employers learned over a hundred years ago either to conform to the regulations imposed upon them or to bribe or in some other way suborn those in charge of enforcing them. In any event, they were involved with the outside world.

The corporation has also always had some kind of uneasy relationship with journalists and writers. Businessmen are traditionally regarded unsympathetically. Perhaps Dickens set the style. In 1854, when Britain was at the height of her achievement as a manufacturing power, he published *Hard Times,* a novel about a northern industrial city—Coketown. In the book Mr Bounderby was Dickens' archetypal entrepreneur.

'He was a rich man: banker, merchant, manufacturer, and what not. A big, loud man, with a stare, and a metallic laugh. A man made out of a coarse material, which seemed to have been stretched to make so much of him. A man with a great puffed head and forehead, swelled veins in his temples, and such a strained skin to his face that it seemed to hold his eyes open, and lift his eyebrows up. A man with a pervading appearance on him of being inflated like a balloon, and ready to start. A man who could never sufficiently vaunt himself a self-made man. A man who was always proclaiming, through that brassy speaking-trumpet of a voice of his, his old ignorance and his old poverty. A man who was the Bully of humility.'

No doubt *Vision, Capital, Manager, Fortune,* or *Management Today* would describe the successful Mr Bounderby in somewhat different terms.

Dickens describes Coketown in a similarly unflattering fashion:

'It was a town of red brick, or of brick that would have been red if the smoke and ashes had allowed it; but as matters stood it was a town of unnatural red and black like the painted face of a savage. It was a town of machinery and tall chimneys, out of which interminable serpents of smoke trailed themselves for ever and ever, and never got uncoiled. It had a black canal in it, and a river that ran purple with ill-smelling dye, and vast piles of building full of windows where there was a rattling and a trembling all day long, and where the piston of the steam-engine worked monotonously up and down, like the head of an elephant in a state of melancholy madness.'

What Dickens began in Britain, Zola in France and then Upton Sinclair in the United States enthusiastically followed. The industrial corporation got a very bad time from the writers and in fact from social critics generally. The kind of drubbing they got made companies more sensitive and hostile and therefore more secretive. This in turn made social critics and journalists more aggressive and even more determined to seek out evil, whether it actually existed or not.

They did not have to look very hard. In the early years of this century there was a great deal of exploitation to find. The big corporation, and for that matter the small one too, behaved for the most part in an aggressive, uncaring, exploitative fashion. Very often this behaviour went beyond even the somewhat rough contemporary social mores.

Over the years, however, two things happened. First, corporations either willingly or under pressure started to behave themselves better. Then they began to realise that they needed to engineer more agreeable relationships between themselves and the societies in which they lived. Despite all their efforts, however, these relationships remained ambivalent, and they still are.

For the most part, companies now behave acceptably, although sometimes the old Adam reasserts itself. Anthony Sampson, in his book *The Sovereign State,* has caused considerable distress to ITT by revealing its tortuous, unsuccessful and somewhat naive behaviour in Chile and elsewhere. A few years ago Lonrho, the British-based conglomerate, was publicly made an example of by Edward Heath. With the regularity of the four seasons, each year somewhere some corporation has to go and stand in the corner for bribery, price-fixing, grinding the faces of the poor or a similar offence. With this kind of background and history it would be absurd to suggest that the corporation can always make social relationships with the outside world that are free from recrimination. Over the past few years a series of new factors have emerged to reinforce the traditional suspicions.

For a mixture of reasons, which are now perhaps becoming over-familiar, the corporation is under attack once again—this time from a rather different angle. *Small is Beautiful, The Greening of America,* pollution, environmental control, squandering the world's resources, the oil crisis, the Unctad resolutions on multinationals (now called trans-nationals), the changing status of women, consumer protection, job satisfaction, participation in management, even the questioning of the work ethic—all these are again putting the corporation on the defensive.

The plain fact is that nobody tells anybody what to do any more. The culture of our day is participative, and although corporations were not built to run by consent, they have to try to adapt themselves to the change.

People are a bit better educated about industry, they now know that the corporation creates wealth for the whole community as well as for the people who work in it. Most people like comfort, they like being well off, and they like having a lot of material possessions. They know that business helps to give them these so in one part of their minds they are not antagonistic to industry.

But there is also an unease about all of this. Maybe the price we are paying for our comfort is too high, maybe we are destroying the environment. Perhaps we are using up our resources too quickly. Perhaps we shouldn't be using so much petrol, perhaps we shouldn't all have cars. Some young people—it isn't clear how many, but at any rate an influential number and far more than ever before—don't necessarily accept the idea that work as such is worthwhile. Interestingly enough, this seems to be particularly true in Britain and Holland, the countries in which the puritan work ethic first clearly emerged.

Perhaps the most dangerous manifestation of all this is that within the past ten years in many Western countries there has been a drift of better qualified graduates towards careers in the social services and away from industry. If this continues, and there hasn't yet been much sign that it is slowing down, and all the best people go into social work and all the duds go into industry, it won't be long before industry will be unable to produce the wealth required to finance the social services.

Today it is fashionable among the young to engage in worthwhile and socially orientated activities. Looking after mentally and physically handicapped people is demonstrably doing good. At a pinch, even being involved in educational and urban planning problems is acceptable. But making money out of manufacturing and selling, say, toothpaste somehow seems frivolous and in a way unworthy—an irrelevant way of passing one's life.

What's more, many of the trappings with which industry surrounds itself are unfashionable. The way businessmen dress, the hierarchical nature of their offices and even the language they use—words like profit, turnover, labour force, canteen—are in many ways alienating to young people.

In addition to all its other problems, the corporation has to consider this situation and make urgent, sympathetic and, so far as possible, appropriate gestures in response.

The corporation has all of the old problems and a lot of new ones too. In a world that is increasingly participative, the ideal corporation would behave appropriately. It would go about its business and make money, but it would not be concerned only with profits. It would have to care for its employees and show that it cared. It would, of course, have to be careful not to care too much or it might be accused of being patronising and paternalistic.

Today a box of chocolates adorned with a picture of the bearded patriarchal founder would no longer be an appropriate gift for the children of a worker celebrating his quarter-century with the firm. Indeed, this kind of gesture would probably be regarded as counter-productive.

The corporation would also care (but not too much) for its employees' families. It would provide work that was not only well paid, but that also provided job satisfaction or, as the German language rather less elegantly but perhaps more accurately puts it, that humanises the working place —Humanisierung des Arbeitsplatzes. The ideal corporation would make products that the consumer would want to buy, that would not be meretricious and flashy, but that would on the contrary be worthy and worthwhile. It would advertise them in a truthful and accurate fashion. The effluent from its factories would be disposed of efficiently without causing offence and preferably at no extra cost, or at any rate without causing the consumer to pay more.

The ideal industrial corporation would also be a good neighbour both locally and nationally, and it would never put its own interests above those of its host nation. Where it had problems it would expose these to the government and try to work out a solution to them in conjunction with it.

Finally, the enterprise, as anticipated in the British Bullock report, would be managed in a democratic and participative fashion by groups representing all levels of the company.

Such corporations have of course never existed, do not now exist and never will exist. Somehow or other, though, corporations are going to have to move in this direction— and perhaps more important, they are going to have to be seen to move that way.

If young people and perhaps other parts of society are alienated from corporations, there are also plenty of corporations that are isolated from many currents in society. Some companies today are utterly bewildered, they really aren't sure what is expected from them. What are they supposed to be doing? If they don't make enough money they are inefficient. If they do make a lot they are greedy. If they are only concerned with their own affairs they are isolating themselves from the community and society as a whole. If they become deeply involved with society they are accused, like Fiat, of trying to manipulate it. Some of the problems the corporation now faces are genuinely very difficult to resolve.

For example, many jobs in factories are boring, repetitive, noisy and unpleasant. It is very difficult for anybody to get job satisfaction from them. An equally difficult problem is consumerism. Consumer groups are, and will probably continue for some time to be, unrepresentative of consumers as a whole. The unpalatable facts appear to be that many and perhaps most consumers, far from rejecting meretricious and flashy products, actually quite like them. And while there is no doubt plenty of room for the sober, well designed product that fulfils all the criteria of the consumerists, there is also room, probably a lot more room, for the perfectly adequate product which is marketed in a standard way—that is to say through a web of truth, half truth and sexual and social innuendo. After all, what other ways are there to market shampoo and soap powder?

Although the debates are taking place in boardrooms, so far very few companies have really moved much. There is plenty of lip service being paid to the ideas of caring, participation and consumerism, but there are very few companies that have significantly modified their attitudes and behaviour. Some companies have, however, moved a long way along certain lines.

As a response to the consumerist movement Carrefour, the huge French supermarket chain, has introduced a number of household products under its own brand name, packaged in a somewhat austere fashion, in terms of both design and material, at prices well below the normal for the kind of article involved. Carrefour is making an attack on the heavy advertising of consumer products for which it claims the housewife in the end always pays.

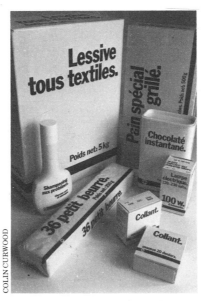

Carrefour's 'non-brand' packaging

Carrefour says that brands with fancy names implying fancy results through fancy advertising cost fancy prices, and Carrefour can help to keep the prices down by cutting out all the extras. Carrefour's brand is a kind of Non-Brand. This is a very interesting and apparently successful attempt by one organisation to harness some of the motivations that have led to consumerism. Carrefour's pioneering efforts have inspired many imitators, including International Stores in Britain.

Equally interesting and indicative of a real change in management attitudes have been the experiments conducted, initially in Scandinavia, on what are now called job enrichment programmes. A job enrichment programme means making a nasty job less unpleasant by varying its content so that it becomes more interesting.

Although they were not by any means the first nor have they been the most successful, the best known of these, presumably because it was the most publicised, has been the job enrichment programme launched by the Volvo vehicle company of Sweden. The Volvo job enrichment programme, which has involved the construction of vehicles in teams, thereby making the job more interesting even if production is rather slower, derived from the need of the company to reduce its previous appallingly high employee turnover.

Although the story has been so widely publicised and perhaps somewhat exaggerated in the telling and retelling that one might be forgiven for regarding it as a public relations exercise, the truth is that both in Volvo and also in other companies, including Saab, these experiments have formed the basis for real changes inside factories.

BOC, the international British-based gases and engineering company, has also made attempts to manifest the change that has come over its boardroom thinking. BOC is keen on participation and it has a number of activities in which worker participation is actively encouraged. Some of its buildings only emerge as a result of discussions between the architects and the people who are going to live and work in them.

Similarly, recommendations for improving drivers' working conditions only emerged after the consultants had spent considerable time travelling with the drivers on their daily runs.

Within BOC, the management believes that its most important asset is people, and that looking after these people can only be effective if they are properly consulted and feel involved in any changes that might occur. The chairman said in 1974:

'Boards and managements throughout the Group fully recognise that the protection of the interests of those who work for the Group is ultimately to act in protection of those who finance it. The key must lie in improved two-way communication between shopfloor, management and boardroom, and back again, and this we must achieve.'

Most corporations, however, have only come to terms with the rest of the world to the extent of placing self-glorifying advertisements in newspapers. These advertisements are sometimes breathtakingly naive. It is fortunate for industry that nobody has so far compared the prestige advertising of, say, half a dozen major companies with their actual behaviour. Whitewashing, particularly when it is self-applied, is rarely very convincing.

These half-hearted attempts to mislead are not in themselves significant, but what they represent is: they are a clumsy attempt to ride out a fashion.

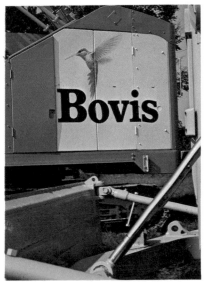

Bovis—a corporate identity with some charm and humanity

So far as the visual identities of companies are concerned, there has for the most part been little change during the past 10 or 15 years. All the traditional aggressive tribal markings with which companies have surrounded themselves in the past—the war paint they have put on to terrify the outside world—have remained almost untouched.

Typical of this is the case of Standard Oil of New Jersey. It is quite extraordinary that Jersey Standard, which is in the course of changing its brand name from Esso to Exxon world wide, at what must be an immense cost, is substituting one piece of meaningless and coarse graphics for another. The design programme created for Exxon is hardly any different from the one the company used when it was called Esso. It says nothing about the company or its relationships with people. It gives no indication that within the past generation the world has changed a lot and companies have to adapt to change. It makes no concessions. It is particularly ironic that Jersey Standard has let this opportunity pass because it has used a highly imaginative and flexible piece of symbolism in various manifestations over some years—the Esso Tiger.

Exxon—a corporate identity that missed its chance

Why is it that the tiger is inferior to the company symbol in the minds of the decision makers in Exxon? Is it because it is only a piece of point of sales material and lacks the dignity of the symbol? Whatever the reason,

Exxon has ended up at a cost of millions of dollars with just another design that says nothing to anybody about anything except 'This is me, here I am. Aren't I big?'

This obsession with size and power is unfortunately significant. All the talk in the world about being friendly, open and approachable is belied by this kind of symbolism. Today, when T-shirts and car stickers—and indeed even ladies' underwear—bear a wide variety of messages—when graphics speak—the tiger could have been Exxon's opportunity to meet the people. The fact that Exxon missed it indicates that the board of directors doesn't truly understand the movements that are taking place in society and that will have a profound effect on the corporation.

One relatively large company that has produced a popular design programme is Bovis. The Bovis company is in civil engineering and construction. It is trying, with who can say how much success, to improve the quality of life on the building site, to make people work more effectively and to co-operate more. Its design scheme, based on a humming-bird, is not simply picked out delicately on an executive's tie; it appears on helmets, working clothing and T-shirts.

Bovis site workers put stickers of the humming-bird on their cars, not because they are asked to but because they think they look nice and they want to associate themselves with the company. The design scheme is popular in the sense that people like it. It tries to show without crudely saying so that Bovis does care for the environment, is committed to managing by consent, and wants to be involved with the rest of the world outside the organisation.

So far, however, not many companies have followed the Bovis example and even within Bovis it has not been implemented with total enthusiasm. It is a sad reflection on the corporations and on the designers they have employed that, with a very few exceptions, all the ferment, all the change in pace, direction and attitude, have passed corporate design by.

Today corporate design is for the most part as stiff, sullen, aggressive and self-glorifying as it was 10 or even 20 years ago. If corporations are changing in their response to society, the way they present themselves visually has to change too—and quickly.

Chapter 7
The search for the corporate soul

'In the first or heroic period of a company's development the personality of its founder gives it its identity. In the second or technocratic phase the carefully cultivated and developed corporate identity is the major element that provides this link. It becomes the substitute for the personality of the entrepreneur.'

If Colin Chapman continues to develop Lotus cars with the commercial and engineering flair that he has so far shown, and if Lotus manages to survive the frosty economic climate of the 1970s, this may be regarded as Lotus' greatest and most heroic period. A new and well equipped purpose-built factory in Norfolk produces a range of high performance luxury sporting cars in limited numbers, while racing machines remain leading participants in Grand Prix contests. The whole thing is still small enough to be controlled by the great man himself. All this is a clear indication that these are the Golden Years of Lotus.

What makes Lotus so attractive is that it is all of a piece. It springs from the talent, energy and determination of one man. Everything about Lotus cars—the products themselves, the way they handle on the road, the way they look, the way they are sold, the way the company behaves to its dealers and to its final customers—is in the end determined by Colin Chapman. The corporate identity of

KOKON CHUNG

Lotus—the result of one man's dream

the Lotus company is implicitly and explicitly controlled by him. You can take it or leave it, but you can't ignore it.

In a completely different sphere, Jack Cohen's Tesco stores chain was also immediately recognisable in its heyday in the 1960s. The only thing that Tesco and Lotus had in common was that they were first-generation companies dominated by men with strong personalities who ran their businesses with immense personal conviction and pride.

Tesco self-service stores and supermarkets sold the same groceries as their competitors at more or less the same prices. But Jack Cohen's stores reflected his background and early years of training as a street trader. They had a certain breezy vulgarity that was recognisably

The old Tesco—street market trading writ large

authentic and attracted a certain type of shopper. The goods in Tesco shops looked a bit cheaper even if they weren't, and the shops themselves seemed to be more agreeable places to go to even if they were a bit scruffier, or perhaps even because they were. The Tesco style, which was idiosyncratic, unpolished and owed nothing to professionals—that is professional marketing men, accountants, systems men, designers or management consultants—made its crude but powerful appeal because it was seen to have a genuine character, a genuine corporate identity, which emanated, of course, from its founder.

Today the business has become much too big for one man to handle, Jack Cohen has now retired as Sir John and the technocrats have moved in. The old rugged Tesco personality has disappeared and Tesco is becoming just like any other supermarket chain. Soon it will be so bland that it may need some professionals to come in and give it a corporate identity.

In the first generation, company style almost always derives from the personality of the founder. Even in the aircraft industry, which has moved from the entrepreneurial to the elephantine stage in about 70 years, there are still one or two elderly relics who maintain the individuality and the independence of their companies. They have ignored the lessons provided in Britain by the late Sir Frederick Handley Page who kept his company out of the mergers forced on the industry by Duncan Sandys. While he lived, the company survived; after his death, however, Handley Page simply fell to bits.

Marcel Dassault, the aged French aircraft manufacturer, is regarded, even by those who dislike him intensely, as by far the greatest military aircraft constructor in Europe and possibly in the world. The series of Mystère and Mirage interceptor aircraft that have emerged from Dassault factories since the early 1950s have been technically brilliant. The methods by which they have been designed and constructed have certainly aroused admiration and envy, even though the way they have been sold and to whom has raised a few eyebrows.

Until the mid-1970s Dassault wielded absolute power in the company. After a series of scandals and commercial misadventures SNIAS, the French national aerospace company, and Dassault formed a co-ordinating committee. Nobody doubts that in the long run Dassault will lose its independence; it will no longer design, build and sell products with its traditional flair. It will no longer be surrounded by an atmosphere of mystery and scandal. The name Dassault may well linger on as a brand name for some part of the Aerospatiale empire, but its magic is already going.

Huge businesses in particular usually go through an heroic period. There is a first-generation drama in which the style and personality of the company are very clear— when the founder creates and then builds up the organisation largely in his own image. Then, when the founder retires, whether they are in aircraft or cars or soap or retailing, such companies move rapidly from the entrepreneurial into the technocratic phase. Inevitably they both gain and lose something. Put simplistically, they lose flair and personality and they gain stability. A whole series of skills have to be substituted for those of the founding genius. Marketing men, production men, corporate planners and regiments of technocrats move in, unhappily sometimes to correct the wilder excesses in which the entrepreneur may have indulged during his last years.

The technocratic phase must begin with big changes. Sometimes the entrepreneur will not go until it is nearly too late, even just before the twelfth hour has struck. Occasionally he leaves behind an appalling mess. William Hesketh Lever nearly destroyed the soap business he had built up. Even when this does not happen the tycoon leaves behind him a system that only he can really manipulate and understand. So with the best will in the world the company has to change. Over a period of years the new managers develop an organisation that inevitably has a different and more subtle character.

In its first period the corporate identity of the organisation emanates directly from the founder. But in the technocratic phase of a company's development, its corporate identity has to be cultivated very carefully because the company's personality is no longer as clear as it once was.

This is not to say that it no longer has a personality, or that the corporate identity of a company in a technological phase of development is a wholly artificial creation. What it does mean, however, is that such a corporate identity is less natural and intuitive; it is more carefully contrived and developed. The corporate identity must now be carefully related to the company's long-term and short-term objectives. Corporate identity can help to achieve these objectives in terms of recruitment, share price, community relations and marketing. The corporate identity of a company in the second phase of its development is a management tool. It is used to sharpen and give point to the personality of the company and help it in achieving its corporate objectives.

In the first phase the personality of the leader of the company is the identity. He holds the organisation together and gives it its style, for better or worse. He controls the way it behaves, the way it looks, the way it speaks, what it produces and how it does its business. In the second phase the corporate identity, if carefully planned, carefully thought through and effectively related to the overall strategy, is the major element that can provide this link. The carefully cultivated corporate identity becomes the substitute for the personality of the entrepreneur, just as the carefully planned marketing policy is the substitute for his intuitive feeling for what the market wants.

If it is to mean anything, the corporate identity must say something about the organisation that is intrinsic to its personality. It is not true that all big companies are the same—they aren't. Some are very dissimilar.

Some companies are about marketing, others about manufacturing—or buying or selling or accountancy. It's glib, and in most cases not wholly accurate, to say that industry is only about making money. Many companies are primarily interested in what they do and only secondarily interested in making money out of it.

Many mature organisations manage to develop an ethos, a way of doing business, that is so characteristic and so much a part of them that they seem to pursue it relentlessly, almost regardless of who runs the company. These companies have a personality which is so ingrained, so much a part of them, that the corporate identity expresses itself in their every action.

An interesting example of this is Daimler-Benz. Daimler-Benz is obsessed by its own technology. The company is in business to make the best product it can and of course to make a profit at the same time. So if in the manufacture of a car there is a choice between a cheaper technical process and a more expensive and better one, Daimler-Benz will usually choose the latter. Because Daimler-Benz wants to make high quality products it has to choose the best processes. This helps it build better products, which in turn enables it to charge higher prices. The higher prices mean higher margins on each vehicle sold. This means more money available for research and development and for better processes, which in turn means even better vehicles at even higher prices.

The whole thing becomes a self-fulfilling prophecy. The soul of Daimler-Benz lies in its technological obsession.

All of the visible manifestations of Daimler-Benz underline this. It does everything with an apparently maniacal perfectionism. Naturally, by some strange process of osmosis, the three-pointed star of Mercedes has come to represent the company's technological supremacy, even though it is intrinsically meaningless.

In a different sphere, Rank Xerox, the highly successful company concerned with marketing Xerox equipment throughout much of the world, is dominated by the idea of selling. In the jargon of our day, it is selling-skills orientated. Xerox in the US develops the equipment and Rank Xerox has no real interest in technology. Its growth and its success have depended on its ability to exploit markets. The soul of Rank Xerox is in selling.

Marks & Spencer, the British owned and managed equivalent of the American Sears or J C Penney is, on the other hand, buying-skills dominated. Even its greatest admirer couldn't accuse Marks & Spencer of having highly developed marketing skills. What it is really good at is seeing that the food and clothing it gets from its suppliers is better quality and better value than the stuff the supplier puts out under its own label, and that the products sold under the St Michael label are better value and higher quality for the same money than you would get elsewhere. The soul of M & S is in buying.

Sometimes the soul of a company is elusive because it is changing its role. Organisations like Unilever's United Africa Company, Harrisons & Crosfield or the French SCOA (Société Commerciale de l'Ouest Africain) are metamorphosing. At one time they were commercial operations within the British or French imperial structure, exporting expensive finished products from the home country and bringing back raw materials from the Empire.

Today all this is changing. The companies are adjusting themselves to operate in the Third World, which may be the same place as the Empire geographically, but is totally different emotionally. They are also changing their pattern of operation to car manufacturing and a whole variety of other activities, including retailing. That is why they are changing their names—United Africa Company has become UAC International, for example, as part of an attempt to adapt itself to a new form of business life.

Even among the world's biggest oil companies there are marked differences in personality, as Anthony Sampson describes in his book *The Seven Sisters:*
'The seven companies shared these same international opportunities and limitations, as they

had grown up together, with their network of joint ventures and consortia closely interlocked. But each of them saw the world with a different perspective, influenced by its own needs to sell or buy oil; and each still bore the marks of its own history, and lived partly in "the long shadow of its founder".

'In New York two of the sisters face each other across 42nd Street, but with almost opposite viewpoints; Texaco ... cultivates a reputation for meanness and secrecy, while Mobil over the road is the most loquacious and extrovert of them all, churning out explanations, complaints and counterattacks through the TV channels and newspapers.

'Across the Atlantic in London, the headquarters of BP rises up from its own piazza, announcing with its name Britannic House that here is an oil company that is part of the nation's patriotism, half-owned by the government.

'Exxon, like many other multi-nationals, is full of the rhetoric of global responsibilities; it likes to stress that it serves not only its American shareholders but all the nations where it operates.'

Elsewhere in the book Sampson describes the elegant New York headquarters of Exxon:

'Up on the fifty-first floor ... the atmosphere is still more rarefied. The visitor enters a high, two-storey lobby with a balcony looking down ... on the vulgar bustle of Sixth Avenue. But in this elegant setting, the directors themselves are something of an anti-climax. They are clearly not diplomats, or strategists, or statesmen; they are chemical engineers from Texas ... It is in Texas, not New York, that the Exxon men feel more thoroughly at home; and it is the Exxon skyscraper in Houston, the headquarters of Exxon, USA, which seems to house the soul of the company.'

Sampson says of Shell:

'Across the Atlantic another oil city presents itself as a world organisation, with a style more lordly and sedate. On the South Bank of London, looking over the Thames, is the great Shell Centre ... The decor suggests an obsessive introversion, as if devised by a crazy conchologist: shells on the glass doors, shells along the façade, an exhibition of sea-shells in the lobby and a high sculpture in the courtyard which turns out to be made up of shells.'

'Shell men nowadays like to apologise for the building's pomposity, but it may have some symbolism; for it suggests not only the self-containment, but the overwhelming importance of Shell in the economy of the home country—an importance even greater in the other half of its home, in The Hague. Shell men regard Exxon as a provincial company.'

About Gulf, Sampson writes:

'Over in Pittsburgh, the headquarters of Gulf convey the unique character of the company, a huge, self-contained family firm.'

All of these companies are inevitably restricted and confined in terms of the visual aspects of the corporate identity they present. However closely British Petroleum wishes to associate itself with the national interest, it knows that it would be commercial suicide to present itself, say in France or Germany, as British.

Equally, however mean spirited Texaco may be, it has to look clean, bright and attractive to its publics.

Shell, which despite its cosmopolitan history and background is totally obsessed with itself, reveals this in the way it has practically taken over conchology and in its constant fiddling with the way it presents itself.

It is Mobil, however, that Sampson feels is most concerned with communications and has tried to do the most to distinguish itself from the others. Mobil launched a major visual identity programme under the direction of the late Eliot Noyes, who in turn chose other consultants to work on aspects of the programme. The eminent New York consultants Chermayeff and Geismar are responsible for graphics. During the past few years Mobil has completely redesigned its graphics, petrol stations, pumps and the uniforms of attendants. It has made great efforts to break away from the stereotypes laid down by its competitors and collaborators and to create a different style for itself.

Mobil has used corporate identity to distinguish itself from the competition and to reveal its corporate personality. Mobil is trying to win approval. Its service stations are as well designed as any can be. Its graphics are strong but modest. Its colour schemes are agreeable. Its packaging is powerful but in the best possible contemporary taste. Mobil wants to be a goody. It is trying to opt out of the role of sinister, double-dealing, world dominating giant in which it has been cast along with its six sisters.

The identity programme is only a part of the Mobil communication programme. It seems that wherever there is a newspaper or a television set there is Mobil explaining, instructing, admonishing and arguing. Mobil wants to tell us that it is a useful, effective organisation, providing wealth and generally making the world a better place to be in. Its visual identity programme is part of this theme. Mobil has thought its identity programme through. It is no accident. It isn't a whim. It's all on purpose. And the purpose is to make Mobil better liked.

ERIKA CRADDOCK

More complex, but more common, is the case of the organisation that has grown by acquisition, engulfing one company after another. Some British examples are Cadbury-Schweppes, Ranks Hovis McDougall and British Leyland. In the United States this tendency has been much more marked and even more extreme. The former Swift meat company has embraced so many other different kinds of organisation, ranging from other meat companies to Playtex bras, that it has had to change its name to Esmark.

It is possible, if one looks hard enough, even to find out what makes this kind of company tick. GEC is still a one mind brand, and for that matter a one man band. Behind the intricate facade of names, styles and activities Sir Arnold Weinstock's attitudes and obsessions are those of the company. Presumably Sir James Goldsmith's Cavenham also operates very much in his own style.

Certainly Harold Geneen's ITT is even today dominated by his particular style, manner and interests.

Many other companies formed by mergers and takeovers are still suffering from such violent indigestion that the only ambition they have, let alone style or soul, is to avoid choking to death. But somehow or other even in the most complicated company there will be something that motivates it—that is more powerful and more idiosyncratic and personal to the company than anything else.

When the management style is set by a dominating figure like Harold Geneen or Sir Arnold Weinstock, or for that matter Colin Chapman or Marcel Dassault, the corporate personality, or if you like the corporate soul, emerges without too much help from formalised corporate identity programmes because it informs and infiltrates every part of the corporation's activities.

Similarly, when an organisation is not dominated by a person but by an idea, an obsession—technical excellence, say—its identity will also emerge clearly throughout everything it does.

For the most part, though, the soul of the company is less clearly visible, its attitudes more compromising, its interests broad and very complex. Companies like this need the formal disciplines, structures and assistance that a specially prepared corporate identity programme can provide.

Chapter 8
Corporate identity as a management tool—organisation

'The main problem some companies have to face is the extent to
which the imagery of the organisation as a whole obliterates,
dominates, endorses or is endorsed by its component parts.'

Marks & Spencer has a simple shape and it stays that way. For the most part it sells products called St Michael in shops called Marks & Spencer. It doesn't make the things it sells. Although it's getting bigger all the time it does so by doing more of the same.

IBM is a bit more complicated than Marks & Spencer, although it's still only in one group of businesses and uses a single name. It makes electric and electronic machines, peripherals and software under the name IBM.

IBM and Marks & Spencer are typical of companies whose activities are relatively easy to comprehend. They do one thing or a group of closely related things using one or two names. Into this category more or less come companies like J C Penney, Volkswagen, Kodak and Sainsbury's.

At the opposite end of the spectrum come companies that do all kinds of things. What does ITT do? Pretty well everything, apparently. This is how it described its activities in its 1975 Annual Report.

'Today ITT's most important businesses are in the basic markets of Telecommunications, Insurance/ Financial Services and Natural Resources. These areas with stability and potential for the long term accounted last year for over 80 per cent of our consolidated net income.

'In addition, ITT's other industrial and consumer businesses include many areas with potential— electronics, foods, components, consumer goods and industrial products, for example. They too have excellent prospects, and with the application of research and continued entry into worldwide markets, form a fourth cornerstone for progress.'

This fairly straightforward, simple sounding observation sweeps across such a network of companies, countries, activities and brands that it is practically impossible to comprehend without the closest possible scrutiny. Just to take a few examples: in telecommunications equipment ITT makes telephones, cables and various types of switchgear under a whole variety of different names, each of which is well known in national markets. In Britain, for example, it's called STC (Standard Telephones and Cables), in Germany SEL

(Standard Elektrik Lorenz) and in Norway it's Standard Telefon og Kabelfabrik. ITT owns Hartford, the American insurance corporation. In what it calls its Natural Resources activity ITT has a multitude of companies including Rayonier, a chemical cellulose organisation, and Pennsylvania Glass Sand Corporation, which produces a wide variety of materials used in pharmaceuticals, glass, cosmetics, polishing compounds and practically everything else you can think of. Within ITT's lawn and garden material resources activity comes O M Scott & Sons. In food products, ITT has Continental, a leading producer, and its own Morton Donut shops. ITT also owns Rimmel, Payot and Ashe cosmetic products, and Sheraton Hotels.

In fact, under the leadership of the dynamic Harold Geneen, there is hardly any business that ITT has kept out of. So while it's relatively easy to get an idea of the shape of Marks & Spencer, it's very difficult to get any idea of the shape of ITT.

In between ITT on the one hand and IBM or Marks & Spencer on the other are those companies whose expansion is dictated by some kind of production or marketing logic. They stay, broadly speaking, in the business of baking or building or bending metal, but they move backwards, forwards and sideways, sometimes in a rather bewildering way. If they are in biscuits and cookies they move into chocolate and candy. If they are in chocolate and candy they move into biscuits and cookies. If they are in heavy engineering they move into light engineering. If they are in light engineering they move into heavy engineering. Sometimes they move unpredictably: one big engineering firm recently went into pizzas, although it didn't stay in them long.

The world's great chemical companies have made moves into pharmaceuticals, fertilisers, paints, magnetic tape, fibres, agricultural chemicals and foodstuffs in addition to churning out massive quantities of chemicals for other people, often their own competitors, to use.

Companies of this kind often have complex problems of identity. Different groups of people will want a shorthand to describe them. In the City of London and on Wall Street, on the world's stock exchanges, and amongst the international business and financial journalists there will be a desire for categorisation. 'What are you?' people will say, 'An electronics company? A chemicals company? A rubber company? A conglomerate? A capital goods company? A consumer goods company?' Each of these descriptions is loaded with significance. Each of them goes in and out of fashion. A few years ago everybody wanted to be a conglomerate. Now nobody wants to be one. Today chemicals may be in and electronics out, but next year it might be different.

So if a company is involved in a lot of different things it needs some kind of shorthand to explain to people what it does, because nobody takes the time and trouble to listen for very long.

In the absence of any clear and consistent explanation it will generally be assumed that the company still does what it has always done. So Spillers is the flour and bread company. P & O runs luxury liners. British Oxygen is British and makes oxygen. TI makes steel tubes. This is one major identity problem from which this group of companies as a whole suffers.

Then there is a whole set of problems relating to companies that have been acquired. To what extent should they be seen as independent and to what extent as part of the totality of a group? How much does it help, say, Tube Investments if its subsidiary Raleigh Cycles is seen to be a part of it? Will TI shares go up? Will it help TI to get a better type of recruit for its marketing operations? Will it help TI to establish some of its other brands, such as Creda domestic appliances, in markets where Raleigh is well known? Or is there no real advantage?

Conversely, how much will it help Raleigh if it is closely associated with TI? Will it sell more bicycles? Does TI have some kind of magic ring of quality as ICI does in a different field? If it hasn't, might it at some time in the future? Could it perhaps be a disadvantage to Raleigh? Will the management of Raleigh find itself drawn into discussions with trade unions on national pay deals for the TI group as a whole, for instance? Is the ethos of the TI group so closely related to research and development on steel tubes that Raleigh, an organisation primarily concerned with consumer durables marketing, has nothing to learn and nothing to contribute to the group except in financial terms? To what extent will an overt association between the basic manufacturing units of the company— like Tubes Ltd and Accles & Pollock who supply not only to companies within the group, like Raleigh and Creda, but also to competitors of Raleigh and Creda—affect the business of these basic manufacturing units?

How important are all of these TI brand names anyway? In bicycles alone there is not only Raleigh but also Carlton, BSA, Hercules, Humber, Phillips, Moulton, Norman, Rudge-Whitworth, Sun, Sunbeam and Triumph, not to speak of Wright Saddles, Sturmey-Archer Gears and some other bits and pieces. In consumer durables the main brands are Creda, Russell Hobbs, New World and Jackson but TI also has others. Is it important to keep them all, or some of them, or would it be better to concentrate entirely on one name? Would it be possible or even desirable to use one brand name throughout the whole group's products, ending up with, say, a Raleigh cooker?

Where do group functions begin and end? Is R & D a group function, is personnel, is marketing, is export? Or are these not group functions at all but part of the individual businesses?

What would be the effect on the organisation of leaving the individual units to continue operating separately, and what would be the effect of linking them? A structure in which subsidiary companies are treated as separate units encourages independence.

This is the fundamental stuff of which complex corporate identity problems are made.

Let's look at another example. Joseph Rank started a flour mill in Hull in 1875. He was a prudent man and a capable miller and over the years he bought a number of other flour mills. His expansion policy was pursued by his successors and eventually Rank's company became the biggest millers in Britain. In 1962 it merged with Hovis McDougall and formed Ranks Hovis McDougall. Hovis and McDougall were also milling and baking companies, each with a series of satellite companies and brands.

At about the same time as it had bought Hovis McDougall, Ranks went on a buying spree. In order to secure outlets for its flour it took over many family baking businesses all over Britain, each with its own name and local reputation which Ranks did not change. Ranks also acquired a large number of agricultural merchanting businesses.

In 1968 Ranks bought a foods company, Cerebos, which itself owned a mass of subsidiaries.

By the late 1960s RHM had 570 registered companies of which 291 were trading. It had some well known brand names like Hovis, Bisto, Paxo, Saxa Salt, Cerebos, McDougalls flour, Energen, Scotts oats and Chesswood mushrooms. It also had well over one hundred different bakeries, each with its own local reputation. In addition, RHM owned a whole series of agricultural merchanting companies, some of which had their own range of satellites of various kinds. On top of all this RHM had collected an assortment of motor body builders, motor distributors, finance houses and some even more remote and extraneous activities.

Thus far the RHM story is fairly typical. A successful entrepreneur becomes a dominant force in a particular field. He buys up competitors but keeps them going, partly so that he shouldn't appear too monopolistic and partly because he thinks their names are worth something. Then, as the company grows, it buys backwards into raw materials suppliers—in this case the merchants—and forwards into the final manufacturers—in this case the bakers. It keeps all of them going separately too—after all, it doesn't want to spoil good businesses. Then, just for good measure, it buys into a separate but apparently closely related business—in this case foods.

There comes a point when somehow or other all this becomes very difficult to manage. You can't get any real economies of scale when you run hundreds of separate companies, even if they are roughly broken down into divisions. You can't get effective management development policies. You can't get people to use central services like marketing, research and international co-ordination, or even to understand what they are for. You get waste on a huge scale.

Equally, you can't get people outside the company to understand how big it is, what it does, what it's all about.

Within RHM there was general agreement that there

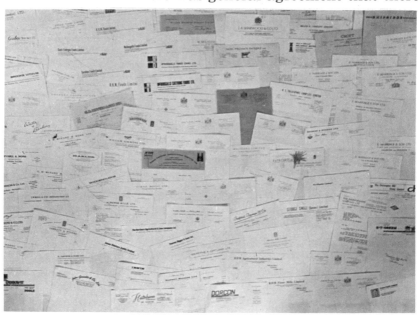

The letterheads of a few RHM companies ...

had to be rationalisation and co-ordination. As part of the programme of rationalisation, consideration was given to the overall identity of the group, the divisions, the companies within the divisions and of the brands.

RHM wanted to create the idea in the minds of the financial community, business journalists and marketing people, that it wasn't only involved in the slow-moving and unglamorous world of flour and bread, but that it was also engaged in more exciting activities. This implied a reorganisation and rationalisation of the names used in the group to give a greater emphasis to those names relating to packaged goods and a lesser emphasis to those concerned with bread and flour.

RHM had a further problem. It was associated with the other Rank, the Rank Organisation, a much better known company. Quite frequently it was assumed that the Rank Organisation controlled or even owned what was thought of as poor old fuddy duddy RHM.

So on the one hand RHM was regarded as unexciting and somewhat dreary—not a glamour company in the eyes of the stock exchange or potential recruits from the marketing world. And on the other hand it was thought to be associated in some sort of subordinate way to the rather raffish Rank Organisation. It had managed to get the worst of both worlds.

The basic problems concerned the company's overall

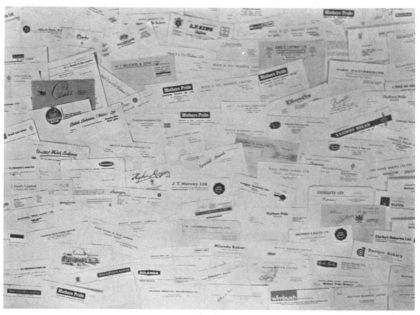

... and a few more

management policy, but part of the resolution of the problem involved a change of identity.

Here are some problems that had to be discussed. To what extent should the companies within the organisation be identified as part of Ranks Hovis McDougall? Were there too many companies in the organisation and should some of them be merged into bigger units? To what extent, if at all, should the brands be associated with one another, and the organisation as a whole? If the company was to look less committed to milling and baking, should it eliminate Hovis and McDougall from its name? If it just called itself Ranks or Joseph Rank, would it look even more closely associated with its better known cousin, the Rank Organisation? So should it change its name completely? Should the main divisions of the company be more clearly identified in order to make it clear that the company was not only involved in traditional milling and baking activities? If the main divisions were identified, where and to what extent should this identity manifest itself, on vehicles, factories, offices and brands? If on the brands, to what extent—as a sign-off or more boldly? In other words, aimed at the direct customer or to the final consumer? If it was decided to identify each of the divisions, should their status as separate cost and profit centres be underlined or should their subordination to central authority be emphasised?

Although RHM did eventually develop a corporate identity, it was reluctant, perhaps understandably, to pursue the problem in real depth.

The RHM case reveals a problem of corporate identity, but not so much in relation to style—what should RHM look like, feel like, behave like—as in organisation. How could some kind of shape, some kind of organisational framework, be constructed for this immense mass so that it looked and behaved in a coherent and effective way?

The RHM case is a typical example of how corporate identity can help to solve organisational problems.

Corporate identity deals with two different but often interrelated problems—organisation and style. When a company, however big it may be, is simple in terms of the things it does, like a Marks & Spencer or an IBM, then the identity problem is basically a matter of style, of putting an image across. When, however, an organisation has a complex mass of businesses or brands or both, some of which are closely and others loosely interrelated, and when many of those businesses have their own powerful identities within particular markets, the identity problem becomes much more complicated. It isn't that style no longer plays a part, it's simply that the part it plays is no longer quite so dominant, and that almost inevitably the organisational problem dominates the style. The main problem this kind of complex company has to face is the extent to which the imagery of the corporation as a whole obliterates, dominates, endorses or is endorsed by its component parts.

Endorsement—making a perfectly ordinary product seem better by associating it with a corporate name that has an excellent reputation in another sphere—is an advantage that a good, clear corporate identity can bring with it. Whether Dulux is a better paint than its competitors is perhaps very difficult to judge; the fact that it comes from ICI may, however, make it appear to be so.

ICI is not alone among the world's great chemical companies in using its imagery in one sphere to push products in associated fields. All of the big chemical companies use their corporate names to push a whole spectrum of different products, some of which appear to the customer to have no links with one another.

The development of a corporate identity system for a complex corporation with maybe hundreds of companies and brands, some with a powerful tradition and very strong loyalties, is a very difficult business and requires considerable skill.

When an organisation, for whatever reason, takes the view that apparently independent brands and companies should be put together to form one coherent whole without losing their individual strength, then it is taking a decision that affects not only its identity and its imagery, but also its reality.

There will be eventual repercussions everywhere. Perhaps there will in the end be fewer companies, and therefore fewer managing directors. People don't like losing their titles, so that can cause trouble.

Perhaps the decision will force people to take some unpalatable decisions about marginal brands and marginal business activities that they have previously somehow been able to avoid. Perhaps it will bring sharply into focus the relationships that various units of the company have with each other. If it's really international and really has world-wide views, why are its overseas subsidiaries so different in their culture, both from one another and from the home company? What about harmonisation of manufacturing methods and manufacturing standards throughout the group? If the image is to be the same, or at least interrelated, what repercussions should this have on the product? Are products using a common name and a common design to have a common performance, or should local standards continue to apply?

The application of a corporate identity programme concentrates the mind wonderfully—as Dr Johnson said of the man who was to be hanged in a fortnight—on a whole series of issues and not just on the identity itself.

When a complex organisation has carried out a proper corporate identity programme it is never the same again. So many issues are raised and dealt with that have previously been avoided, and so many really significant matters have to be thrashed out, that the process in some senses changes the organisation.

Organisational corporate identity programmes of this kind in which the graphic design content comes so much at the very end are not often brilliant, or indeed even very interesting, visually.

Corporate identity, when used as a management tool in a corporation with a series of complex and interrelated companies and brands, poses such intricate organisational problems and imposes such tight disciplines that the visual style that emerges is almost always heavily constrained. That is one of the reasons why corporate identities of major companies have such marked similarities.

Many of the organisational problems of corporate identity that graphic designers are brought in to resolve are beyond the scope of the graphic designer to answer—they require management decisions. But the tools for resolving these problems are handled by graphic designers, who quite often don't really understand the implications of what they are doing.

If RHM, or for that matter BOC or Delta Metals or Lucas or any other major company, decided that it needed to have strong independent divisions, then one way of underlining that decision would be to give each division a different colour. That is not a design decision; it is a management decision. If, on the other hand, the corporation wanted to emphasise that it was tightly controlled from the centre it might well decide to make all divisions look very similar, in which case perhaps only one colour would be used throughout the company's corporate material.

It is this kind of management factor that affects the design programme. Naturally, at the end of it all there will be a set of graphic components that go to make up a visual system—a symbol maybe, a colour or colours, a typeface or even an alphabet. The system has to work in a wide variety of different sizes, materials and geographical and emotional contexts.

Maybe it has to occupy a subordinate role on a well known package goods brand, and a dominating role on an industrial product. Perhaps it must be powerful and glittering on a neon sign, restrained and dignified on the chairman's letterheading (although I'm never quite sure why). It must work when printed crudely on bits of cardboard and in a glossy catalogue. It must be equally suitable for a village shop in Northern Nigeria and a showroom in Bond Street or on Park Avenue. The design scheme must be appropriate for the largest and best known company in the group which might have a name consisting of three initial letters, and equally suitable for the newly acquired subsidiary in Pakistan, which might have a four-word name using Urdu script. The design scheme must be simple and robust enough to be readily understood by semi-literate signwriters in Orissa in Eastern India, but it must have sufficiently powerful stylistic nuances to act as appropriate sign-off to a French TV advertising campaign. It's a bit of a tall order, isn't it, for some colours, a bit of a type and maybe a little mark?

That doesn't mean that these big organisational corporate identities do not have a characteristic style—P & O does look quite different from say, Lucas or Delta, but the style that they have is inevitably dominated by the organisational aspects of the job.

One of the most powerful characteristics of an organisational corporate identity programme is that it has a very powerful tendency to centralise and to make things look the same. It reduces idiosyncracy and it homogenises.

Its strength is that it makes the organisation more aware of itself, more cohesive and more comprehensible. But this is also its weakness in that it tends to inhibit originality and eccentricity.

That's why Colin Forbes of Pentagram, who has worked on a number of major design programmes, has said:

'Somehow or other the logistics of the thing sometimes take over the original concept.'

The real point surely is that very big corporations have to be so many things to so many people. They have to be, or they think they have to be, ubiquitous and omniscient, so the style of the job emerges as a result of these constraints.

Virtually all of the major identity programmes that have been trotted out over the years as brilliant examples of how to do it—IBM, Mobil, Olivetti, Braun, Container Corporation of America, London Transport—relate to simple problems of identity. The companies themselves may well be enormous, but the range of activity, the number of names of brands, and of separate units involved is usually small. The examples almost invariably relate to cases in which the style has been able to dominate the organisational problem.

Occasionally, however, it happens that a company with a very complex organisational problem—a problem as acute as RHM or as TI—can produce a solution that is as elegant stylistically as it is organisationally.

British Oxygen had grown up in the gases business. Like Linde and Messer Griesheim in Germany, Aga in Sweden, L'Air Liquide in France and Air Products, Union Carbide and Airco in the United States, it sold gases to the

Delta and Lucas—organisational corporate identities

steel industry and to a mass of smaller users. It had also expanded into related business like welding, metals and cryogenics. Geographically it had business in most countries of the old British Empire.

In the late 1950s and early 1960s its comfortable position had been attacked officially by the Monopolies Commission and commercially by the American Air Products company, which came into Britain and took a small but profitable slice of its business.

After a short period of shock the company responded vigorously. It needed to do a number of things, all more or less at the same time: fight back against Air Products, make people inside British Oxygen behave in a more commercial and dynamic fashion, regain the confidence of the financial community, and regain the confidence of customers. At the same time the management decided to expand very rapidly, both geographically and in terms of acquisition.

What it all boiled down to was that within a very few years a new management wanted to create a much larger and more successful international business based on a different ideology and to some extent an allied, but more diversified, technology.

The British Oxygen attitude was that companies, wherever they are, should look after themselves and adapt themselves to local situations as part of the life of the country they are in. So companies very often have large, even majority, local shareholdings. In every country the British Oxygen Company has a different name—Canox in Canada, CIG in Australia, POL in Pakistan, and so on.

Clearly, in this light the British Oxygen Company was an inappropriate name for the parent group, so in 1966 the decision was taken to shorten the name to BOC, and

eventually BOC became the name of the European company and BOC International that of the group. Shortly before this a design programme had been introduced. Alan Eden-Green, who had been appointed by BOC to look after Public Affairs, wanted to produce a corporate identity that could be used by all the companies in the group, each of which would continue to use its existing name, and which would work effectively in all of the group's visible manifestations.

Not only were BOC's major companies all over the world using different names, and intending to continue so to do, but the organisation was involved in a spate of acquisitions. Many of these acquired companies were to retain their own names, a clear part of the growth programme being that acquired companies should continue to have maximum autonomy. On the other hand it was agreed that it was desirable that they should feel part of BOC and be seen to be part of it.

The design programme is somewhat uneven in its execution when judged against the highest possible design standards, but it has the great and simple merit that it allows BOC to express itself vigorously, both collectively and as independent units. It allows for the most delicate nuance in terms of individuality, but no company, however independent, can lose sight of the fact that it is part of the BOC organisation.

When BOC went into Brazil it introduced its scheme to its new associate HIME, now called Brasox. It did the same in Nigeria with its partner Van Leer, now IGL.

BOC knew it was changing and it wanted an image change to match. It has managed to avoid subordinating the elan and dash of the revitalised BOC to the very real organisational requirements implied by rapid growth.

Chapter 9
Corporate identity as a management tool—style

'Style can help a company to sell more for higher prices, or to recover its morale, or to project a clearer personality—or all these things.'

IBM operates under a single corporate name in a range of closely related activities. Although its market share varies in different fields and in different countries, IBM has a huge slice of the market in everything it does and everywhere it goes. By any standards IBM is extremely successful. Amongst its readily recognisable characteristics is its style.

The most striking characteristic about the IBM style is its ubiquity. IBM people have it, IBM products have it, IBM buildings have it, IBM brochures and advertisements have it. It's quite clear what the style derives from and what it's about. IBM is simply trying to be the best. Wherever it is, whatever it's doing, IBM wants to be top.

Naturally a company that wants to be the best has to look the part. So it is part of IBM's style that it employs the best designers.

IBM doesn't have ordinary buildings, it buys the best architects and then encourages them to put up the most advanced buildings. Everything it does looks, and is, expensive. In the conventional modern idiom it's the best you can get. All this chrome, glass, steel tube and landscaping must be done for some reason. What is it?

IBM products, whether they are office equipment or computers, have a cachet. Even IBM carbon paper somehow looks more impressive than its competitors'. Our experience tells us that IBM carbon paper is just carbon paper, but our emotions tell us that IBM carbon paper is heavy with IBM know-how, so we don't mind paying extra for it.

Who knows if IBM is the best? Maybe in certain fields its products are better than the competition, but it's difficult to believe that IBM equipment is better than everybody else's all along the line. And yet, somehow or other, if it's got that IBM mark on it, it has to be top.

IBM charges more for its products than its competitors. That can't be an accident. Its margins, so far as one can tell with complex leasing systems, must be very high; certainly its profits are huge. It would appear in IBM's case that style helps profits.

Does IBM get any other tangible benefits out of its style? Well, obviously IBM thinks so or it wouldn't do it, except perhaps that it is so used to it—after all, it's been doing it for over a quarter of a century—that it no longer knows how to do things any other way.

Another reason must be that the late Eliot Noyes, IBM's respected design consultant, had a direct and close contact with Tom Watson Jnr, for many years the head of the company, and this obviously powerfully influenced the way in which IBM behaves. If that's the way the boss wants it, why, that's the way it's going to be.

Then again, its corporate identity programme has helped IBM consciously to cultivate elitism.

IBM elitism not only affects what customers think of the company and the product, and what potential recruits think of the company, it also affects the way suppliers behave. To be a supplier to IBM is quite an achievement; naturally, if IBM wants it, it has to be good and it has to be delivered on time.

Naturally also, the elitism extends to staff. Anyone working for IBM, and particularly anyone representing IBM to the customer, has the whole crushing burden of IBM's imagery sitting on his head. The customer expects something special from IBM; so the man who services IBM products has to arrive on time, look clean, be polite and do the job as well as he can. Elitism makes these demands on him; elitism makes him respond.

The whole IBM ethos is based on principles that have been practised by the British Brigade of Guards for several hundred years—set the highest standards, demand the highest levels of performance, create an atmosphere in which people think they are better than anyone else and they will believe it and perform accordingly. IBM uses style to make itself more effective. And it is.

No two organisations could be more different from each other than IBM and British Rail. IBM is used to winning and being on top; for years British Rail had been used to losing and being at the bottom. Since the 1920s Britain's railway system had been quietly decaying. Over the years it had failed to compete with road transport. It had made no money, it had been neglected, starved of good people, of investment. Like so many other railway systems, British Rail had become a cross between a national joke and a national disgrace.

When Richard Beeching arrived at British Railways in 1963 he was given one clear and overriding brief—that the railway system should be made into a sensible and viable competitor to air, sea and road transport, for the carriage of both goods and passengers. He had to drag the railways into the middle of the twentieth century.

This was an awe-inspiring job. Not only was everything out of date, from the equipment to the system, but, much more important, the people on the railways felt defeated and cowed—decadent heirs to a great Victorian legacy. There were plenty of good people around, but Beeching had to make them realise their own worth. Beeching had no chance, however dramatic and drastic his plans, if the people in British Railways didn't believe in him and in themselves. Beeching had to try and make his customers, the travelling public and the people who sent freight by rail—a high proportion of the population of the country—feel that British Rail was no longer a sick joke.

Unprofitable branch lines were closed. Money was poured into fast container services and high-speed Intercity passenger services. Electrification schemes were undertaken. Huge financial investments were made.

The reality was going to change and very fast. Beeching realised that, as the reality changed, he had to

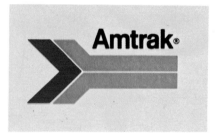

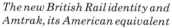

The new British Rail identity and Amtrak, its American equivalent

change the imagery with it. He had to change the style of British Rail. He realised that the changing image would act as a catalyst in changing the reality. Under the direction of the late George Williams, who was made design manager of British Rail, he launched what was probably the most far-reaching, ambitious and expensive corporate identity programme carried out in Britain.

The design programme was so vast that it would have been impossible for one outside consultancy organisation to cope with it and, in fact, a number of design companies were used. Williams commissioned Milner Gray of the Design Research Unit, one of the leading organisations in Britain at that time, to carry out the bulk of work. Work was started in 1963 and is still going on in practically every design field—architecture, uniforms, rolling-stock, brochures, timetables, notepaper, cutlery, crockery, advertising and signs.

The design programme has been carried through at a time when British Rail has been shrinking, when it has been losing huge sums of money, when there have been turbulent labour relations and, above all, while it has passed through successive management and organisational changes.

Bearing all this in mind it has been a considerable success. British Rail now looks, behaves and is treated as part of a twentieth-century transport system, which is as much as anyone can reasonably expect.

However much it wanted to, British Rail couldn't shake off its legacy; the visible manifestations of the organisation remain for the most part Victorian. King's Cross and St Pancras stations obstinately refuse to look modern despite the new signing systems. Desperation with the obtrusiveness of the past led British Rail into a clumsy brutality when it first started to develop its new corporate identity. It was so keen on showing itself as part of the present and future that it tried to pretend the past didn't exist. It was this kind of over-reaction that led to the destruction of a number of magnificent pieces of early railway architecture, particularly perhaps the Euston Arch. Today it looks as though British Rail may be learning its lesson.

Another failing of British Rail in design terms, and a mistake that very many organisations make, is that it seems to have used its design programme in an unimaginative way. A symbol that looks appropriate on a sign doesn't necessarily look right on a menu card.

The British Rail programme is not often shown in books on design—in its application it is too messy, too cluttered, too closely linked with the past, too much of a compromise. In fact, the self-appointed design critics tend not to admire it because it is too much a part of real life. There are many aspects of British Rail's design work that can reasonably be criticised, but in the main it is a superb achievement in helping the organisation to change its attitudes and behaviour by adopting a different style.

British Rail's problems, although they existed on an elephantine scale, are by no means solved. Any huge industry based on a long established and apparently old-fashioned, or at least unfashionable, technology is in the same position. In almost all major countries the railways have faced difficulties in imagery not dissimilar to those of British Rail. The Amtrak programme in the United States is designed to do very largely the same job for parts of the US railroad system.

But parallel problems and parallel solutions can be seen in fields that are apparently quite remote. Bulmers, for example, had totally to change the image of cider and cider drinking before the drink started to become fashionable in Britain. It achieved this cleverly through a mixture of advertising and packaging.

The old established firm of Dennis Bros, builders of specialised transport equipment, fire engines, ambulances and refuse vehicles, has been brought back from the brink of disaster by a new management team. Here is how *Truck* magazine describes it:

'Those of you who knew the old-style Dennis will remember rather grand Victorian premises with a broad stone staircase, green tiles, Doric pillars and all leading to dark, wood panelled, almost Dickensian offices. That's all gone. In its place builders, fitters, plasterers and joiners are busy putting together a modern administration centre to fit the 1980s rather than the 1918s . . . But those are just outward signs of the new-style, highly profitable Dennis.'

Style, visual style, appearance, can play a significant part in changing the way an organisation behaves, or in making its new activities look more credible.

Reeves, the London artists' materials company, is about 200 years old. For most of its history it was in the hands of one family who developed the company's activities in the educational market and among amateur weekend artists. Hardly a child in Britain grew up in the 1950s and 1960s unaware of Reeves products. In the early 1960s Reeves, with the help of its marketing consultant John Gordon, decided to capitalise on its experience and knowledge of children and move the company into the rapidly developing leisure field.

Reeves had a reputation for making worthwhile products. The company knew that a good reputation in the new markets depended partially upon the maintenance of its reputation in its traditional markets.

The new Reeves operation depended on translating the company's style and reputation from one field to another. Glossy packs with nothing much inside would have destroyed Reeves' reputation as a provider of good, honest value. Reeves packaging had for the first time to be designed to sell on its merits, but it had also to look as though it came from the same old Reeves that mums, dads and their children knew and loved.

Reeves launched a series of products ranging in price from a few pence all the way up to pounds in carefully graded steps, utilising existing products and materials but packaged to give the products more sales appeal.

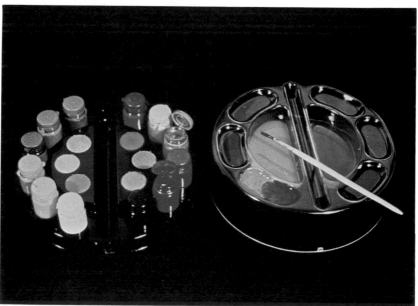

Continuity was also important so far as Reeves representatives were concerned. Good salesmen, even though they may not be intellectually clear about the company and its products, have strong and uncannily

KARIN CRADDOCK

accurate emotional feelings about where the company and its products stand. They know whether or not a product fits into a company's range. Since the company was moving into new fields that Reeves representatives might readily consider somewhat unsuitable and even degrading, particular care had to be taken to maintain the quality, continuity and style of the company in its new packaging.

Many of Reeves' new ranges were not successful straight away. One is, I think, always suspicious of the 'then they lived happily ever after' stories.

Reeves went through traumatic and dangerous times during which its management changed. In the end though, under Wilfred Cass, a brilliant company doctor with a few scars from other and perhaps even bloodier battles, the company's new policy was successful. It merged with Dryad, another company in a complementary field, and eventually, when everything was going well, as is so often the way of these things, Cass sold it to a much larger group, in this case Reckitt & Colman. Since Reckitts, like Unilever, tends to operate through brands, it seems unlikely that the Reeves style will change in the immediate future.

Winsor & Newton, like Reeves, makes artists' materials, and it too has now fallen into the open mouth of Reckitt, but in the days of its independence Winsor & Newton also had discussions with a well-known designer about its corporate identity in general and specifically about a range of inks that represented a very small proportion of its business, but whose sales it wanted to expand.

Michael Peters, with whom Winsor & Newton dealt, is basically a retail packaging designer, and he tends to think that corporate identity and packaging have a very close relationship. He also believes that corporate identity is, or should be, about selling. The fundamental premise that he proposed and that Winsor & Newton accepted was that the products should sell because they were attractively and idiosyncratically packaged and that the packaging, each individual item of which might be quite different from any other, would collectively add up to a range. The provisos were that the new packs should not cost more than the old packs to make and that they should have international recognition and appeal.

Since its introduction, the new range of inks has increased sales by 600 per cent. Customers now buy the whole range. Peters says that the inks were designed for creative magpies who collect sets. Since the phenomenal success of the inks Peters has moved on to other ranges of Winsor & Newton products.

The Winsor & Newton programme is an interesting step in the development of corporate identity as a marketing tool. It takes a company and instead of creating a logotype, a symbol and a series of colours for the company name and its related brands—instead, in fact, of attempting to homogenise the impression that the company makes— it does precisely the reverse. It makes each object produced by the company look different. It even writes the company name in different styles. But through the original and exciting themes it uses throughout the programme it creates a unity that emerges from the diversity.

Winsor & Newton has been bold—it hasn't copied anybody else, it hasn't pushed its name and logotype in the usual ritualistic fashion, and it has implied in its identity that it both knows and cares about the business it is in. The implications of Peters' work for Winsor & Newton in developing individual variations of an overall corporate identity are profound.

There is probably very little difference between the products of Winsor & Newton, Reeves, Rowney and most of the other artists' materials manufacturers in Japan, Europe and the United States, but it is more than interesting that two of them in this quite small industry have adopted new and quite different corporate identity programmes that have been commercially successful.

A change of style helped another medium-sized British manufacturer. In the British meat pie and sausage market, as in so many other fields, everyone follows the leader. In the old days the leader was Wall's, a Unilever subsidiary. Wall's dominated the industry and everybody imitated and looked like Wall's, including a Wiltshire manufacturer with big ambitions called Bowyers.

Bowyers' management and its then advertising agency, Vernons, felt that the company would remain at a disadvantage if it continued to look like a reach-me-down Wall's. Bowyers' products, like Wall's, are designed to satisfy the broadest English taste, so almost by definition it is unlikely that one company's products will taste markedly different from another's. Equally inevitably, apart from the occasional 'startling reduction', there is unlikely to be much difference in price between one company's product and another's. If Bowyers was to differentiate itself, to make itself more attractive to the consumer and sell more sausages and meat pies, it would have to do it through all the paraphernalia of marketing, including advertising, packaging and product identity, because no other means were available.

There was no question here of dealing with the soul of the company or of its organisation or structure. The problem was related strictly to making the company and its products look more desirable to the customer. But within these overall requirements there were a number of significant technical constraints that had the effect of determining the nature of the style.

For example, in shops the products were usually displayed in cold cabinets in which they were difficult to identify, so by implication the name Bowyers needed to be big. The Wiltshire address of the company was thought to be a good selling point since it had associations with the more agreeable aspects of pigs, nature and the countryside. The design programme that was produced actually had the effect of making the company look much older and more traditional than it really was.

This raises an interesting question: is the Bowyers programme a brand identity or a corporate identity? The main difference between brand identity and corporate identity is that a brand identity is directed outwards towards one audience—the final consumer—whereas

How Bowyers imitated Wall's, the industry leader ... and then developed

corporate identity has a number of different audiences, both outside and inside the organisation.

By that definition Bowyers is a brand identity; it was created to make a specific impression on final consumers, it was not designed to help a new management turn a company round or create a new feeling of commitment. Nor was it devised to change the atmosphere, impress the City of London, help recruitment, improve relationships with the local community or raise productivity. It was simply part of a marketing programme—created to help sell more sausages and meat pies—and it did.

The role of corporate identity in Bowyers, Reeves and Winsor & Newton was quite straightforward: it was to help with marketing, to help the companies make more money. The job that was carried out was simple and cosmetic.

IBM is perhaps the classic example of a company using style in real depth to help every aspect of its performance—to make money, to recruit effectively, to buy well and to create good community relations. In the case of British Rail, or Amtrak, or Dennis Bros corporate identity has served another purpose: it has been used to help change the

...a new generic style which the rest of the industry then followed

atmosphere so that a lot of things that were wrong could be put right and so that people both inside and outside the organisation could see that things were being put right.

One of the reasons why both Amtrak in the United States and British Rail have leaned so heavily on corporate identity to make them look modern and competitive is that powerful design schemes are a distinguishing feature of many transport systems, especially airlines. In fact, their corporate identity programmes are the only things that distinguish many airlines from one another.

All over the world, airlines use the same equipment; 727s, 737s, 747s, DC9s, DC10s and Tristars fly to the same places in the same time. The airlines charge the same prices and serve the same kind of food in the same way, no matter where they come from.

The International Air Transport Association, the trade body to which most of the world's major airlines belong, governs the distance between seats, the amount and type of food to be served (there was once a long controversy over what constitutes a sandwich), and a whole series of similar minutiae, as well of course as dealing with more important matters like how much the fares should be for various journeys. If, by some freak of good or bad fortune, one or two airlines happen to get some kind of temporary marketing advantage—for example, British Airways and Air France have the Concorde which, whatever its other disadvantages may be, does actually get there quicker— then IATA regards this as unfair competition to the airlines that haven't bought Concorde and they make Concorde passengers pay more.

In this Alice in Wonderland world, corporate identity is about the only thing that airlines have left to maintain some kind of individuality. They can't sell price, it's the same; they can't sell service, it's also the same; they can't sell comfort, that's the same too. They can sell destination and departure time, but nobody is going to fly to Miami just because PanAm tells them to, or even because National says you can fly Rita.

They are driven into a position in which the only way they can distinguish themselves from one another is by the way they dress up. In the case of national airlines like KLM, Alitalia, Lufthansa and British Airways, almost inevitably their identity becomes some kind of crude travesty of one or more national stereotypes.

So Alitalia has to make up its mind whether it is Mama mia, spaghetti bolognese and arrividerci Roma, or whether it is Michelangelo, Florence and Verdi. Air France has to decide whether it's ooh-la-la, Gay Paree, Brigitte Bardot and not tonight Josephine, or the Loire Valley, Normandy, quenelles de brochet, Monet and the Comédie Française.

And because the potential customers of Alitalia, Air France and all the other airlines come from so many different places, expect so many different things, and travel for so many different reasons, the airlines are reluctant to adopt even a national identity wholeheartedly.

For the holiday traveller they feel they ought to look quaint and interesting; for the business traveller they like to look efficient; for the nervous traveller they want to look reassuring and familiar; and of course for all travellers they want to look friendly.

The mess Alitalia has managed to get itself into is effectively illustrated by this quote, which comes from an article in the airline's own in-flight magazine *Flytime*.

'Before Alitalia there was Marco Polo. And Vivaldi, Julius Caesar and Rodolfo Valentino. Let's admit it, we have tourism in our blood. There's no city in the world that hasn't at least one Italian restaurant or an Italian musician.

'And there are a lot of Italian engineers and technicians around too. A point we would like to stress, just in case you imagined our country was only *sole, pizza and amore.*'

Apart from Sophia Loren, Benito Mussolini, Enzo Ferrari and the Bay of Naples, Alitalia seems to have shoved in the lot.

Alitalia is not the only culprit: if British Airways says it takes good care of you but it's always on strike, then patently there's something wrong somewhere. If friendly Air India stewardesses spend more time chattering to each other than answering the passenger's call button, then they are manifestly not as friendly as Air India says.

Brand imagery isn't enough for an airline. The identity and the style have to go all the way through the organisation and be projected internally at all levels as well as to the outside world. The airlines' problem is that most of them confuse their brand image—that is their image to the single audience of the passenger—with their corporate identity—that is the way in which they should look and behave to all of their audiences. They could all learn something from IBM.

Airlines, like banks, petrol companies and indeed very many suppliers of products and services, know that they don't differ very much in the fundamental aspects of their business. They sell approximately the same thing at about the same price and give much the same service. The main characteristic that distinguishes one airline or bank or one petrol company from another is its personality, the way it presents itself, its identity.

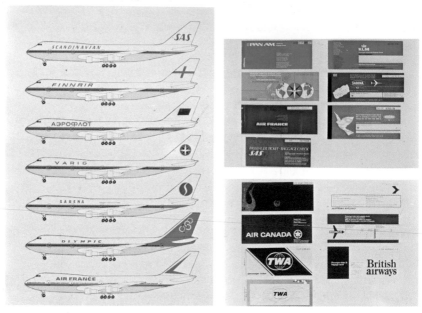

Airline corporate identities show no spontaneity or originality

Style—the creation of a new appearance—helped to restore some kind of self-confidence to British Rail. Style— outward style and not much else—helped Bowyers to make itself more competitive in the meat products market. Style— a thorough, deep-rooted style—has helped IBM to achieve and maintain its place in the world's electronic markets.

The marketing director of one of the world's major heavy vehicle manufacturers told me that he felt that all the big truck companies made equally good products. He said that one company might get a minor technical advantage for a time, but the business was so tough that it didn't last— the competitors soon caught up. In his view the only real difference between the major manufacturers was in their respective images.

This view strikes at the fundamental belief of engineers in the triumph of technology, with which they confused the idea that people always buy the product that is the most suitable for the job.

The decision to buy a piece of capital equipment is a complex and sometimes heavily formalised, even ritualised, process. It involves both rational and irrational factors.

Apart from all the rational factors that are taken into

consideration—the quality of the equipment, its price, the service offered by the manufacturer, his reputation—there is also a network of less rational factors, including the personality and style of the people selling and the personal interaction between the buyers and the sellers. So inevitably there are the presentations, the visits to factories and all the other rites between buyer and seller that are the human equivalent of dogs sniffing each other.

The ritual of selling almost all expensive industrial equipment is much the same. It starts with a letter or a phone call from a potential purchaser or a visit from a salesman; sometimes he is called a consultant, sometimes an engineer, sometimes perhaps even Regional Manager Western Hemisphere, but he is always really a salesman. The visit is followed by a deluge of catalogues. There is a short interval and then comes a request for a broad price, delivery date and specification—in other words, a request for a proposal, for a tender.

This is when the serious stuff starts. How is the tender prepared and who prepares it? Is the tender just a technical document or is it also a persuasive selling document? Are all of those who are involved in the decision to purchase going to read it or only some of them? Will all of them want to read all of the tender, and so should it be highly technical all the way through, or should it have some entertaining bits in it such as who else has bought the equipment, how clever the selling company is and what its history is?

Should the selling company spend a lot of money as well as time on the tender to make it look glossy, or should it simply produce the minimum required in a workmanlike but economical fashion?

After the tender, or sometimes before, comes the visit to the factory. Once again, should the company present itself in an austere, sober way, as a jolly, hearty fellow or as Good Time Charlie?

When the potential client visits the factory, the works and the offices temporarily become the showrooms; they are the point at which the product is being sold. In a very real sense then, what the factory looks like—to use the quaint expression that works managers are so fond of, what the 'housekeeping' is like—can and from time to time does genuinely have a direct impact on the decision to purchase. So in a sense factory layout, equipment, maintenance, signing systems and the state of the works lavatories and canteens can all have a direct bearing on sales.

When a company is scrutinised really closely and its tenders, offices, factories and the way it entertains are used to sell, its corporate identity really emerges as part of the process of marketing.

Other things being equal, if one company's product is as good as and no better than its competitors', the sale will be made on a basis that is at least partly irrational.

All of these irrational factors can be summed up in terms of words like style, sympathy and personality. If a company's style is clear, consistent and logical and the potential purchaser happens to like it, then that company will win. If a company's style is confused, confusing and anonymous it has that much less chance. Corporate identity, for the purpose of selling things in the industrial context, is not just bits of paper; it is what a company makes, how it makes it, the conditions in which it makes it and how it sells it.

The corporate identity allows the company to present itself to its potential customers in a thorough way. This is the point at which the real differences in style, personality and soul between one company and another really emerge. This is the point at which consistency, a real self knowledge and a genuine and deep corporate identity help. And this is the point at which, when everything else is equal and there doesn't seem to be anything to choose between the price, quality and service of the product offered, the irrational element in the selling process takes over. If there isn't anything to choose between the equipment offered, am I going to choose IBM or Honeywell or ICL or CII or Siemens computers?

If I want reassurance, and most of us do most of the time, then IBM can give me that. IBM can give me the comfortable feeling that I can't really be making a mistake.

But I may not like the IBM style. I may find it too big, too smooth, too glib, too know-it-all, in which case I might find another supplier emotionally more attractive.

We all make our choice of goods and services for a peculiar mixture of reasons: to suit our egos, because we really think what we are choosing is the best, for convenience, for chauvinism and for both rational and irrational reasons.

The consumer goods industry is much clearer than the capital goods sector about the emotional and irrational appeals its products make. A lot of the advertising for consumer goods is not designed to explain in detail a series of product advantages because these frequently defy explanation—how can you genuinely demonstrate that one brand of breakfast cereal is superior to another and anyway, what does superior mean in this context?—it is designed to create an attractive and agreeable atmosphere around the product that makes a certain emotional appeal to the purchaser. Naturally a lot of people prefer to pay less and buy the 'own brand', as most supermarket chains know, but even so a high proportion of the people who buy, say, lemon squash are happier to buy the brand they know with its attendant emotional appeal.

A lot of research work has been carried out (who knows how much of it meaningful) on the relationship between the package and what goes inside it. Cigarette smokers devoted to Brand A are revealed, in tests where the pack is switched or in some other way tampered with, to have confused Brand A with Brands B, C and D, products for which they have previously displayed the greatest possible contempt.

Even more dramatic results have emerged from research involving drink. When blindfolded, many seasoned whisky drinkers, with years of devotion to one brand, have been found not only to confuse their traditional tipple with other whiskies, but even — presumably after a couple of stiff ones — with gin and other spirits. The legend — I cannot vouch for its truth — is that whisky can even be confused with water when its traditional sensual associations are removed. That is to say when you can't see its colour, can't smell it, can't look at the glass it's in, can't see the bottle and are only left with the taste, the chances are you won't know what you are drinking.

Now I have no first-hand comments to make on these matters. I don't smoke and have never claimed to be able to taste the difference between Teacher's and Glenmorangie. Above all I have never seen the research. I merely offer these observations for what they are worth. It remains for me a legend, like the Russian soldiers, still with Siberian snow on their boots, seen passing through Aberdeen railway station on their way to the Western front in the First World War.

One certain thing, however, is that the atmosphere surrounding the product, the impression the packaging makes through shape, colour and material, profoundly influences what we feel about it.

The elaborate packaging of Havana cigars — the wooden container, the layers of thin paper, the band around the cigar, the complications involved in opening the box — all add to the feeling of connoisseurship and luxury associated with the product. A Montecristo No 3 wouldn't be the same shrink-wrapped in a plastic sachet displayed in a dispenser next to Wrigley's chewing gum and Benson & Hedges cigarettes.

My colleague Michael Wolff shows how dramatically packaging affects the way we feel about a product in some experiments that he has carried out transposing labels. Shown here, with some minor modifications, are the labels of pharmaceutical products and whisky.

What these experiments indicate quite clearly is that the emotional strengths of graphics are such that they can set up very powerful and contradictory irrational feelings.

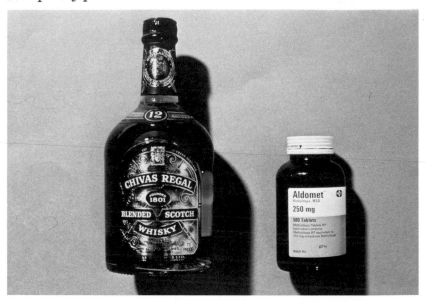

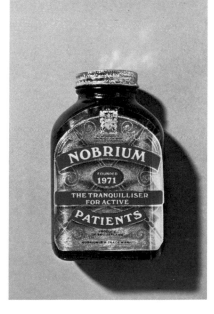

Chapter 10
Corporate identity and brand identity

'Theoretically the dividing line between a brand identity and a company or corporate identity is very simple: a brand is a wholly concocted creation, it is devised solely to help sell and it has no life of its own. In practice though it's all more complicated.'

Question 1:
What do Dulux paint, Sunsilk shampoo, Mr Kipling cakes, Sara Lee cakes, Kitekat catfood and Lux soap have in common?
Answer:
They are all brand names. They were devised as brand names and they never had a life outside the brand.
Question 2:
What do Rover cars, Macleans toothpaste, Johnnie Walker whisky and Pears soap have in common?
Answer:
They were once independent companies selling recognisable products or services. They are now brand names used by large companies to distinguish one range of products or services from another.
Question 3:
What do Heinz, Bang & Olufsen, Volvo and Liberty's have in common?
Answer:
They are all independent companies with a readily recognisable range of products or services that are clearly and characteristically their own.

How do companies present themselves and their products to their customers? Sometimes, as in Question 1, they go off and invent an entirely new name; they dream up brands. There is no 'Mr Kipling', for example, and he doesn't personally make the 'exceedingly good cakes' that the advertising slogan claims. The 'exceedingly good cakes' are made in RHM factories all over Britain by RHM employees. If you want to complain about the quality of Mr Kipling cakes, or for that matter congratulate Mr Kipling on his splendid performance, there will be no Mr Kipling to reply, unless by now some harassed marketing man has invented him. For that matter, there is no 'Sara Lee' at General Foods either.

The brand in its purest form is a figment of the marketing man's imagination. It is the ventriloquist's dummy; the corporate marketing people pick it up and put it down again whenever they feel like it. The consumer may react to the dummy, but the dummy cannot respond by itself; it is manipulated by the company.

Sometimes though, as in Question 2, the corporation doesn't dream up a brand name at all. It buys a company with a reputation for making a particular product and then just develops it.

Beechams didn't invent Macleans toothpaste; a Mr Alex Maclean thought of it and not unreasonably he called it Macleans. Macleans is now, along with Lucozade, Corona, Brylcreem and a number of others, one of the brand names of the Beecham group. The time has long since gone when Macleans was a separate entity with a separate factory and separate staff. Macleans these days, despite its origins, has no more substance than Mr Kipling.

Johnnie Walker, on the other hand, is different. Like most of the other well known Scotch whisky brands, Johnnie Walker is part of the Distillers Company. But it has its own offices, staff, transport fleet and above all a distillery where it produces its own whisky. Kilmarnock is not just another distillery belonging to the Distillers Company, but the Johnnie Walker company base. The policy of the Distillers Company has been not only to maintain the facade of the separate brands for the consumer, but to retain their reality so far as possible. Only in this way, it believes, can it maintain genuine competition in a field in which as a whole it is so dominant. There is therefore a difference in kind between Johnnie Walker and Macleans toothpaste, which is now only some packaging, advertising and a formula.

On the other hand, Johnnie Walker, which is for the most part a real company showing the same face to most of its audiences, is also circumscribed. It is not a reality for the City of London or Wall Street, or for financial journalists. It becomes less of a reality the higher its staff climb the management ladder. At the top, above Johnnie Walker, is the Distillers Company.

There are certainly points where imagery and reality clash. Johnnie Walker's reality collapses at the distribution depot. All the famous whisky companies belonging to Distillers transport their own whisky in their own lorries from a shared distribution depot—a Distillers Company depot. So that early in the morning at a Distillers depot you can see the vehicles of the famous competing brands going out of the same gate together in harmony.

The only organisations that present aspects of the same identity to all their audiences are the ones that don't use brands at all. These are dealt with in Question 3. Heinz, for example, doesn't have RHM's problems. If you don't like Heinz tomato soup, or more probably if you do, you can write and tell the company so. There are Heinz factories, a Heinz managing director, and Heinz representatives selling Heinz products to the trade; Heinz is a real company.

Theoretically the dividing line between a brand identity and a company or corporate identity is very clear: a brand is a wholly concocted creation that is devised solely to help sell and it has no life of its own.

The brand identity is aimed at one audience—the final consumer—but the company identity is aimed at many— the final consumer, the trade, competitors, suppliers, local government, national government, trade associations, trades unions, the financial community, consumer associations, journalists and its own employees of various kinds in different places. Sometimes the company will want to say different things to different people at different times; it may even want to say different things to different people at the same time.

The company develops a way of projecting itself that it uses to communicate to all its audiences, internal and external. The brand identity only looks outside to its audience of the consumer; the identity of the company, the corporate identity, looks both inside and outside at a wide spectrum of audiences who have different views of, attitudes towards, and interests in the company.

In practice, however, all this is modified by circumstances. Often a company spends millions projecting its brands and very little on projecting itself, so the brands seem to dominate the company. Ovaltine, which in some countries is called Ovamaltine, seems almost totally to have obliterated Wander, which is the name of the company that started the brand. Some brands are so successful that they seem to take on a life of their own—Lux isn't just a toilet soap any more, it's become the name for a whole range of products.

Sometimes, as in the case of Johnnie Walker, the brands are not just brands, but quasi-independent companies spawning their own brands—Red Label and Black Label—jealous of their own imagery and anxious to preserve their own way of life. Socially, particularly after thalidomide, it's much better to say that you work for Johnnie Walker than for the Distillers Company.

Sometimes, when a brand name is not properly nurtured and looked after, it deteriorates so that it becomes meaningless. Many of the Leyland names now unhappily fall into this category and so do many of the great British radio and TV brand names from the past.

In the world of radio and television, Rank and Thorn have used the names of their constituent companies in so many different ways at various times that they seem to have little validity left, even as brands. Sony conveys a clear idea, it means something, and so does Hitachi and Bang & Olufsen, but what do Murphy or Bush or Ferguson mean? They are just brand names that have been shuffled about by brand managers, more or less indiscriminately so far as an outsider can see.

The relationship between the brand and the corporation that owns it is a dynamic one. Unless this relationship is constantly monitored it can run into trouble—and it often does.

One way of keeping brands under control is to create a strict hierarchy of names. Unilever, one of the arch-priests of branding, is fairly clear here, as it is in so many other fields. Usually it adopts a three-tier structure: on top there is Unilever—the corporation, never wittingly used for trading companies. Then there are the manufacturing units—Lever, Van den Berghs, Union Deutsche Lebensmittelwerke and so on. Then come the brands—Omo, Rama, Stork and a few thousand others. In this structure the final consumer relates to the brand while most of the people in or dealing with the company relate both to the company— Lever or Van den Berghs—and to Unilever, although the level of awareness will vary according to the nature of the job. The factory worker in an isolated plant will be more conscious of the company, say Lever, whereas the senior executive will be equally conscious of the corporation, Unilever, and the company.

The advertising agency working on a new product will be conscious of the immediate problem, and therefore of the company with which it is dealing—Lever Sunlicht, say— but the opportunities existing throughout Unilever will not have escaped its notice and will no doubt act as a spur. Some Unilever companies only have two levels of operation: in Britain both Wall's ice cream and Wall's meats company present their companies as brands, so do Langnese and Iglo on the European market.

Unilever is disciplined, and above all highly experienced, in the way that it handles brands; other companies are not. There seems to be some lack of clarity among managers of the GEC organisation, for example, about the differences between a brand and a company.

As GEC expanded, it took over the old AEI and English Electric companies, and with them it took over a multiplicity of companies and brands. Neither AEI, the initials of Associated Electrical Industries, nor English Electric had been outstandingly successful in rationalising companies, company names, brands and brand names— which was one of the reasons why both companies fell into the lap of GEC.

GEC took over a network of companies operating in a number of complex ways over a broad spectrum of industry. GEC has made an attempt to extract the benefit from a whole variety of company and brand names, many of which no doubt had considerable significance and goodwill in the past, but the effect, to an outsider at least, appears to have been unsuccessful. GEC doesn't seem to have made up its mind what is a brand and what is a company.

Here is a list of the principal subsidiary companies of GEC in the UK—it comes from the 1975 Report and Accounts of the company. Laid out neatly and tidily it seems to make sense; in advertisements, however, the whole thing begins to look cockeyed.

Principal Subsidiary Companies of
The General Electric Company Limited

The English Electric Company, Ltd
Associated Electrical Industries Ltd
The Marconi Company Ltd*
GEC-Elliott Automation Ltd*

Power Engineering

GEC Power Engineering Ltd (m)
  GEC Turbine Generators Ltd*
  GEC Gas Turbines Ltd*
  Ruston Gas Turbines Ltd*
    Napier Turbochargers Ltd*
  GEC Switchgear Ltd*
    Vacuum Interrupters Ltd* (60% Ordinary)
  GEC Transformers Ltd*
  GEC Rectifiers Ltd*
  GEC Reactor Equipment Ltd*
  GEC Engineering (Accrington) Ltd*

Industrial

GEC Diesels Ltd*
  Ruston Paxman Diesels Ltd* (m)
  Dorman Diesels Ltd* (m)
GEC Traction Ltd*
GEC Machines Ltd*
GEC Woods Ltd* (m)
  Woods of Colchester Ltd
  Keith Blackman Ltd
Birlec Ltd*
Claudgen Ltd
The Express Lift Co Ltd
GEC Overseas Services Ltd
Simplex of Cambridge Ltd (95% Ordinary)

Telecommunications,
Electronics and Automation

GEC Telecommunications Ltd* (m)
  Telephone Cables Ltd* (74.5% Ordinary)
  Reliance Systems Ltd
  Associated Automation Ltd*
GEC-Marconi Electronics Ltd* (m)
  Marconi-Elliott Avionic Systems Ltd* (m)
  Marconi Communications Systems Ltd* (m)
  Marconi Radar Systems Ltd* (m)
  Marconi Space and Defence Systems Ltd* (m)
  Marconi International Marine Co Ltd*
  Marconi Instruments Ltd*
  Easams Ltd*
GEC Computers Ltd
GEC-Elliott Traffic Automation Ltd*
GEC-General Signal Ltd* (50% Ordinary)
GEC Transportation Projects Ltd*

AEI Scientific Apparatus Ltd*
McMichael Ltd*
GEC Medical Equipment Ltd*
GEC Electrical Projects Ltd* (m)
GEC-Elliott Process Automation Ltd*
GEC Elliott Process Instruments Ltd* (m)
GEC Industrial Controls Ltd* (m)
GEC-Elliott Mechanical Handling Ltd*

Components, Cables and Wire

GEC Electrical Components Ltd (m)
  GEC Electronic Tube Co Ltd*
    English Electric Valve Co Ltd*
    The M-O Valve Co Ltd
  GEC Semiconductors Ltd*
  AEI Semiconductors Ltd*
  Salford Electrical Instruments Ltd
  Londex Ltd*
  GEC Measurements Ltd (m)
  Black Automatic Controls Ltd*
  Satchwell Control Systems Ltd*
  Satchwell Sunvic Ltd*
  GEC-Elliott Control Valves Ltd* (m)
  Redring Electric Ltd*

GEC (Cables and Equipment) Ltd (m)
  AEI Cables Ltd* (m)
  GEC Henley Ltd* (m)

The London Electric Wire Company & Smiths Ltd*
  Kent Bros Electric Wire Company & E H Phillips Ltd*
  F D Sims Ltd*

GEC Installation Equipment Ltd (m)
  GEC Distribution Equipment Ltd*
  GEC-English Electric Fusegear Ltd* (m)
  GEC Walsall Ltd

Walsall Conduits Ltd*

Consumer Products

GEC (Radio & Television) Ltd*
Spectra Rentals Ltd (80% Ordinary)
Cannon Industries Ltd*
Osram (GEC) Ltd
GEC-Xpelair Ltd
GEC Schreiber Ltd (62.5% Ordinary)
  Hotpoint Ltd*
  Schreiber Industries Ltd*
English Electric Consumer Products Ltd*

In this advertisement, Marconi-Elliott Avionic Systems is called a GEC-Marconi Electronics Company. What brand is the customer supposed to be buying? Is he expected to talk about GEC-Marconi Electronics, or about Marconi-Elliott, or about GEC-Marconi Elliott, or what?

The next advertisement is for a product called Clayton, which is presumably a brand name of GEC boilers, but GEC boilers is part of the Boiler Division of GEC Diesels. So what does that make Clayton?

In the next advertisement, headed 'Industrious RK', Ruston Diesels Limited is described as a management company of GEC Diesels Limited, which it transpires lives at the same place as Clayton—Vulcan Works, Newton-le-Willows. To further complicate matters in this advertisement, GEC no longer has 'boilers' neatly written underneath GEC and the legend 'Boiler Division of GEC Diesels Ltd'; it has 'GEC' with 'Diesels' written underneath and then, just in case you were in doubt, 'Holding Company —The General Electric Company Limited.'

Industrious RK

Diesel or dual fuel engines from 240 bhp (162 kW) to 5000 bhp (3500 kW) for base load, peak chopping or standby power generation. Ask for full engine data.

Ruston Diesels Limited
Vulcan Works, Newton-le-Willows
Merseyside WA12 8RU, England.
Telephone: 09252 5151
A MANAGEMENT COMPANY OF GEC DIESELS LIMITED

Ruston Diesels Limited

Vulcan Works, Newton-le-Willows,
Merseyside WA12 8RU, England.
Telephone: 09252 5151

A MANAGEMENT COMPANY OF GEC DIESELS LIMITED

HOLDING COMPANY—THE GENERAL ELECTRIC COMPANY LIMITED

GEC wants to use the best of its existing stock of names in such a way as to retain customer loyalty. But it also wants to reduce the number of names and to associate them as much as possible with GEC. All of which is perfectly clear and laudable. But what emerges doesn't seem to make much sense, largely because the names GEC uses have differing traditions and backgrounds that mean very different things to people—customers, agents and employees—and they are being thrown together in a way which reduces them to meaninglessness.

These names are for the most part not invented brand names, but names of proud old companies with long independent traditions. You simply can't expect to sling all of these together and hope for the best. The process of changing a company into a brand is delicate, complex and full of difficulties. It has been very successfully done and it could be done by GEC, but not in the way the company is going about it now.

As a contrast to the confusion of GEC, let us look at a couple of examples of well controlled developments in this field. Carters was at one time an independent garden seed company operating from Essex. It had land on which it grew seeds and it had offices. In the mid-1960s the company was bought, gutted and filleted; the land went in one direction and the product in another. Eventually the name and goodwill, but not much else, was absorbed by Cuthberts, another seed company based in North Wales, which also owned further seed companies called Ryder and Dobies. In order to take advantage of the economies of scale, the Carters operation was gradually integrated into Cuthberts. In the meantime, under the energetic direction of Clive Clague, the chief executive of the group, Cuthberts moved into other fields, some of which were quite remote from seeds. It is now part of the Swedish KemaNobel organisation.

Carters gradually faded away as a company: it didn't buy independently, it didn't grow independently, it didn't pack independently and it didn't have its own independent staff. It became part of the seeds operations of Cuthberts. Now there are no more Carters employees or Carters warehouses and there are no more Carters offices; Carters has slowly evolved into a brand. But it remains, so far as the seed buying public is concerned, a very potent brand because while the company has been withering and dying the brand has been growing and expanding. The identity that projects Carters seeds as a kind of genial, green-fingered, knowledgeable company is a ventriloquist's dummy of Cuthberts, but it seems to the final consumer much more real than the old Carters ever did. Paradoxically Carter's new packaging gives the impression that it is much more of a reality than the old packaging ever did,

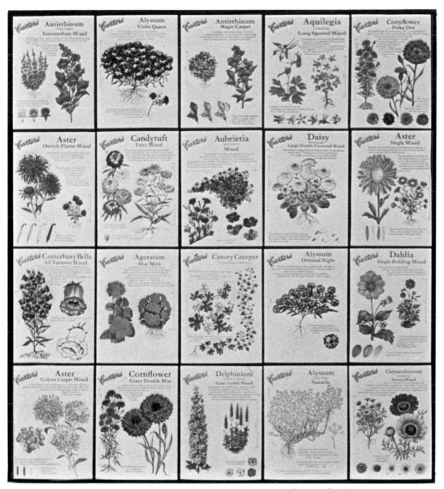

Carters' new packs avoid jargon and try to make gardening easy

with a genuine feeling and interest in its product, while its previous packaging was old, tired and boring. The evolution of Carters is complete.

It is perhaps equally instructive to look at another example which, like a science-fiction creature, is still mutating. The Cunard Steamship Company was at the height of its splendour and glory before the arrival of the jet passenger plane, and its great ships were symbols not just of national engineering skills, of great speed and comfort, but also of international luxury and glamour. Before the Second World War the Cunard Line had absorbed White Star and was busily battling with Holland Amerika, the French Line, the Italian Line, the Hamburg Amerika Line, the United States Line and a number of lesser rivals.

Even in the 1950s Cunard was still doing very well,

but when transatlantic travel by jet aircraft took over, Cunard, in common with the other companies on the route, went into decline.

Like some of the others, Cunard thrashed about desperately to try and save itself. It went into air travel and came out again, it went into containers, it built a magnificent new ship, the QE2, it even went out and got itself a new corporate identity—but the end for Cunard was really inevitable.

Cunard was bought by Trafalgar House, a big, successful property and construction company, which thoroughly reorganised Cunard and put it into profit.

Trafalgar House seems to make a speciality of resuscitating the sick and dying. Within the past few years it has bought not only the Cunard Line, but also the Ritz Hotel in Piccadilly, London, more renowned lately for its architecture than its hospitality, and the Beaverbrook Group of newspapers, whose noisy death rattles have been the subject of gossip over many years.

Although the Cunard offices and showrooms in the West End of London, expensively revamped in its new corporate style in the early 1960s, have been vacated, there is not much sign so far as the outside world is concerned that the Cunard Line is not what it once was. The QE2 still makes voyages to the United States and goes on cruises round the world, but now it makes money out of them.

But clearly Trafalgar House did not buy Cunard simply in order to keep it as it used to be; the name Cunard is being exploited in a variety of new directions. For example, Trafalgar House is operating a new hotel in Hammersmith called the Cunard International. It would be sensible to expect Trafalgar House to use the Cunard name in the future in connection with a series of luxury travel and leisure activities.

So what is Cunard now? Is it a brand name for the leisure activities of Trafalgar House? Is it like, say, Macleans toothpaste with no life of its own? Or is it a wholly owned subsidiary of Trafalgar House that runs ships and has a reality of its own—more of a Johnnie Walker, in fact?

Well of course, the answer is that at the moment it seems to be a bit of both. We can reasonably assume that the seafaring staff of the company still feel that they are Cunard people and certainly the passengers on the QE2 feel that they are travelling with Cunard. Probably the travel agents and most of the other groups of people with whom Cunard deals—suppliers of food and drink,

Cunard's Queen Mary (top left and above) and the new Trafalgar House Cunard International—a hotel with pursers and purserettes .

KARIN CRADDOCK

victuallers as they are quaintly called, the dockyards and so on—all of these still probably have a relationship with Cunard and not with Trafalgar House. But these suppliers are likely to be aware of changes in Cunard management and also of changing attitudes in management during recent years, and they will associate these with the new ownership. So all these people will think of Cunard as a separate company, or anyway an entity. The financial world, journalists and the City of London, however, know that Cunard no longer exists as a separate entity and are curious to see how Trafalgar House will develop it. They think of Cunard merely as a part of Trafalgar House.

When we turn to the Cunard International Hotel at Hammersmith we see another stage in the mutation. This hotel, which opened some years after the takeover of Cunard by Trafalgar House, has a clear brand connection with Cunard but no other. It has model Cunard liners about the place and uses some Cunard motifs here and there.

Cunard is a good name for a hotel, of course, but so is, say, Bristol (another hotel in the Trafalgar House empire). For that matter, Rothschild would be a good name for a hotel too. It is doubtful if the managerial staff of the Cunard International Hotel, let alone the waiters and chambermaids, feel any real connection with the old Cunard company. For them, Cunard is simply the name of the hotel. For guests, however, particularly older American ones, Cunard will have implications of transatlantic travel and of luxury; the brand implications will have been translated from a shipping to a hotel name.

While the QE2 exists and while a separate Cunard operating unit is maintained, links with the old Cunard will ensure that some version of the Cunard identity remains. If, however, Cunard becomes the name for a Trafalgar House expansion into hotels, safari parks, luxury holiday homes and other property/luxury leisure activities of which, like the QE2, the rump of the traditional Cunard activity is only part, then we will have witnessed the mutation of Cunard from a company to a brand.

If brands cause all this fuss and bother, need endless care and protection and monitoring, and so easily get out of control, why do companies bother with them?

Well, some companies don't. Both in the industrial and the consumer field, and particularly in service industries, many organisations use their corporate name for all their activities and find life much simpler that way. But in some industries there are powerful traditions encouraging the use of brand names; in pharmaceuticals, for instance, everybody seems to use them. The idea here is for the medical detail man—rep to you and me—to impress his company's name for a particular brand of drug—Librium, Valium or whatever—on the doctor.

The basis for pushing brand names is that the doctor is so busy that he won't remember the name of the corporation and a description of the drug, so he needs a neat, short name instead. This seems to me to be at best a dubious argument, which puts ethical pharmaceuticals into the same category as floor polish and soap powder.

Precisely the same argument is applied to the housewife so far as domestic products are concerned. The different brands of toothpaste, soap, washing powder and shampoo can, it is thought, best be distinguished from one another by a name that in some cases projects a whole range of qualities about the product—Sunlight, Vim, Nimble, Mother's Pride, Sunsilk and Homepride all carry some kind of promise in their name. But for that matter, Fry's Turkish Delight, Bowyers sausages and Liptons tea all convey meanings quite as specific as the brands with which they compete, but they are not conventional brand names. Like Carters seeds or Johnnie Walker whisky, they live somewhere in the world between the brand name and the company name.

By contrast, each oil company usually presents a

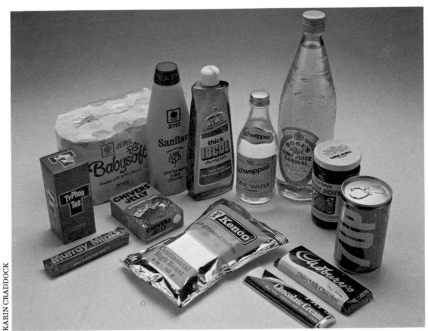

A few Cadbury-Schweppes products—brand names or companies?

monolithic identity wherever it goes and normally in an oil company brands are dominated by the corporation. For the most part, of course, the products of oil companies are homogeneous and lend themselves to this treatment.

The large branded goods companies on the whole take a different view. Some, like Procter & Gamble, have virtually no corporate identity; others, like Colgate or Cadbury-Schweppes are rather less shy, but these two companies don't seem to be able to make up their minds whether they are selling brands or the corporation, and when and to whom.

The reasons why companies in the branded goods field are for the most part so slow, hesitant and uncertain about their corporate identity policy is that they have associated it—and frequently confused it—with marketing tactics for branded goods. Because they spend vast sums of money on advertising their products they have allowed their marketing/advertising policies on brands—which are of course dictated by their need to appeal to the final consumer —to overwhelm all their thinking about their other audiences. Slowly, however, some of the companies are getting some kind of relationship between the corporation and its needs and the brands and theirs.

In retailing there was once a fashion for brand names; large, respected and highly successful companies like J C Penney, the United States retailer, used a multiplicity of different names for their own brands of merchandise. Today, as the retailer becomes increasingly self-confident in relation to the manufacturer, he is tending to present himself less equivocally.

There are still a few hangovers though. What possible reason can Marks & Spencer have for using the brand name St Michael? Does St Michael give the products an endorsement that Marks & Spencer as a name lacks? No. Does St Michael distinguish one quality or type of product from another? No. Does it make the products sound more glamorous or more interesting? No.

The official company reason is that while most St Michael products are sold in Marks & Spencer's own stores some, outside Britain, are sold in other people's stores. But what kind of a reason is that? The products could still be called Marks & Spencer. The real reason must be emotional: the company has used the brand name for a long time, it has grown accustomed to it and it just doesn't like the idea of dropping it.

Where does the brand name and identity stand in relation to the corporate name and identity? It varies enormously: in the case of St Michael and Marks & Spencer the brand name is so weak that it has to be propped up with constant references to the much more powerful corporate name. 'St Michael', the slogan reads, 'the brand name of Marks & Spencer'. This is a far cry from the situation in

which the brand name is much more significant than the corporation. Ask who makes Ovaltine; not many people know the name Wander. Ask who makes Kleenex; Kimberly-Clark is not a name that springs readily to mind. Or for that matter, ask who makes Concorde; most people won't know. The chances are that even Frenchmen and Englishmen won't be able to say with certainty that it's Aerospatiale in France and British Aerospace in Britain.

Marks & Spencer doesn't need any brands, and the Concorde brand has become over-inflated. These are two instances in which the brand has not been properly thought through in relation to the corporation. It isn't so easy to keep a brand under strict control; they have a habit of sliding about a bit and if you don't watch them carefully they can take over—they need constant and careful study.

Equally important is the way that a subsidiary company can slide over into a brand almost without anyone noticing it. Moves take place as a result of, say, the rationalisation of production or the better use of facilities or a change in personnel policy—moves which are not intended to have anything to do with marketing at all—and these can have considerable repercussions on the companies concerned.

It is possible that such a move is happening at the time of writing between Peugeot and Citroën. Citroën is now a subsidiary of Peugeot, but it has been announced that it will continue to operate separately. This may be true, but a

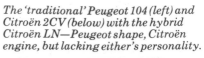

The 'traditional' Peugeot 104 (left) and Citroën 2CV (below) with the hybrid Citroën LN—Peugeot shape, Citroën engine, but lacking either's personality.

Citroën small car has already been announced that looks like a Peugeot but uses a Citroën engine. How long will it take before other parts are standardised between the two car ranges, then for the dealer network to be rationalised and finally for factories to make both ranges? How long will it be before Citroën, almost without anybody realising it, becomes a brand of Peugeot? What will happen then to the Citroën employee? With whom will his allegiance lie? Who will he work for? What signs will be put on Citroën factories? It is problems like these to which the company running brands has to address itself.

The corporation has to know what names it possesses and understand how all of its identities should be most economically and effectively used.

Chapter 11
Names

'There is nothing more emotional and less susceptible to rational
analysis than a name. It requires a major exercise of imagination
to visualise what a company would look and feel like
if its name were changed.'

How would you like to work for a company called
Hamburg Südamerikanische Dampfschifffahrtsgesell-
schaft Eggert & Amsinck? Probably not much, but when it
was formed in 1871 that kind of name was very fashionable.
The Peninsular and Oriental Steam Navigation Company,
which was started in 1840, must have had an agreeably
sonorous sound to its founder directors. A hundred years
ago a company name wasn't the real thing unless it had a
good, comfortable length. Mr Montague Tigg, or Mr Tigg
Montague as he became, Dickens' shady company promoter
in *Martin Chuzzlewit,* had a good feel for a name. He
launched a fraudulent company which he called The Anglo-
Bengalee Disinterested Loan and Life Insurance Company.

'... "What will be the paid-up capital, according to
the next prospectus?" "A figure of two, and as many
oughts after it as the printer can get into the same line",
replied his friend.'

Today Monty Tigg, as he would be familiarly known,
might well be involved with something called Trans-
national Electronic Components, or even European
Electronic Components—EEC for short. The changes in
fashion of names reflect the preoccupations of society. The
Home & Colonial Stores and the British & Colonial
Aeroplane Company were both products of Edwardian
Britain—imagine calling a chain of supermarkets Home &
Colonial today.

Some names go out of date because the concept behind
them doesn't wear very well. Barclays Bank activities
outside Britain used to be called Barclays DCO—DCO
stood for Dominion Colonial and Overseas. Now Barclays
DCO is called Barclays International.

Whereas at the turn of the century everything was
Imperial and Colonial, today it is International and
European. You can find a Euro Advertising, Eurocars
(Citroën main agents), Eurodesigns (architects),
Euroframes (picture framers) and naturally Eurographic
(graphic designers). There's also Europlane, which is just
an idea between a few aircraft manufacturers, Europcar, a
car hire company, and a few hundred more Europ, Euro and
Europas. There is even an advertising agency called, would
you believe it, Intercon. It's very difficult to persuade people

that the 'in' name of today is the 'out' name of tomorrow.

The creative consultant Terence Griffin has created a name bank. A name bank is like a land bank or, for that matter, a money bank: you keep the names in there until you need them. He has created a Japanese motor car company called Mikimakimoto Motors; a cake company called the Marie Antoinette Patisserie (slogan 'Let them eat cake'); and a bomb-site car dealer called Immaculate Autos. His masterpiece is the chocolate manufacturer called the Rococo Cocoa Co.

I once worked for an advertising agency in India called D J Keymer that changed its name three times in just a few years. It had been purchased by S H Benson in London, and it was for a time its sole overseas possession.

Then Benson's began to expand internationally, and we woke up one morning in Bombay and found ourselves called Bomas—Benson's Overseas Marketing and Advertising Service.

Then Benson's full name was adopted by the Indian company, and it became S H Benson (India) Ltd. A few years ago poor old Benson's merged with Ogilvy & Mather and now Benson's in India is called Ogilvy, Benson & Mather, and I am happy to learn that it continues to flourish.

Some company names get so closely associated with a particular product group that it's difficult, or even impossible, to associate them with another one. If Shell bought the Express Dairy from Grand Metropolitan, it couldn't sell Shell milk. Somehow it would taste of oil.

Some countries change their names because of historical associations they don't like: thus the Dutch East Indies became Indonesia and the Gold Coast Ghana.

When a company thinks about its corporate identity its name is sometimes a major part of the problem. For one reason or another the company sometimes outgrows the name. British Oxygen Company, for example, was simply misleading as a name. It associated the company solely with one country, Britain, and one product, oxygen, whereas in reality it was engaged in a world-wide range of activities. Similarly, Ranks Hovis McDougall gave the impression of a company that was exclusively involved with flour and bread. Both British Oxygen and Ranks Hovis McDougall took refuge in initials.

BOC and RHM aren't the only ones with problems: TI has problems too, according to Prufrock, the gossip columnist of the *Sunday Times Business News,* who wrote on 3 April 1977:

'Tube Investments is about to spend £350,000 on London Weekend TV to promote its corporate image ... Apparently research has shown that if consumers think of the group at all, they think of it as grey, diffuse and remote. Tube Investments does not want to be thought of as faceless and unfriendly ...

'The trouble, of course, is that both tube and investments are among the greyest words in the English language. I think all the group really needs to do is change its name. Its own subsidiary Accles & Pollock has shown what can be done in this way. (Remember Tickles & Wallop or Shackles & Wedlock?).

'After careful consideration I have decided on the ideal change: Terrific Industries. Just send me the £350,000. I'll take a cheque.'

Jute Industries of Dundee changed its name to Sidlaw. British Ropes, whose reasons for change were much the same as British Oxygen's, turned itself into Bridon. But the problems facing Jute Industries (Sidlaw), and even the much bigger British Ropes (Bridon), pale into insignificance beside the classic story of United States Rubber. US Rubber began making galoshes in the last years of the nineteenth century. The company grew with the motor industry; it expanded both organically and by acquisition vertically and horizontally. By the middle 1960s it was about number 50 in *Fortune's* top 500 companies.

US Rubber had every possible problem related to names that could afflict a multinational. Its full name, United States Rubber Company, implied that it was a company making rubber products in the United States. But of its 33,000 products many were neither made of rubber nor made in the United States, so just as it stood its name was misleading.

A much more complex and immediately difficult problem faced it in the tyre market. In world terms there are only a dozen or so major tyre manufacturers—Goodyear, Firestone, B F Goodrich, Dunlop, Pirelli, Michelin and a few more. Each of these companies uses one name wherever it goes, so if a Ford car built in Germany with German-made Michelin tyres is sold in Britain, those tyres can be replaced with the same kind of British-made Michelins. In another context Dunlop, say, could, if it chose, rationalise its production, making all its heavy vehicle tyres in France or India. Rationalisation of this kind has obvious and major benefits.

In a world-wide industry in which products come from different places and go to different places, many companies eventually feel it's just that much more efficient to use a single name. Inevitably it's very important that the name doesn't conjure up adverse associations. Well, US Rubber had plenty of plants overseas with its own name, like US Rubber Mexicana, but it found that its popularity was uncomfortably closely linked to that of the US government. When the United States did things that the locals didn't like, the US Rubber plant got it in the neck too.

In addition to the plants it ran under its own rather constricting and misleading name, US Rubber also owned a number of well known, big, rapidly expanding companies with powerful regional reputations. Of these perhaps the best known was Englebert which was an old established Belgian rubber company well known within Europe, where it had a number of plants. But US Rubber also owned Dominion in Canada, North British in the United Kingdom and a few more.

US Rubber couldn't compete effectively with the Dunlops and Firestones and Pirellis, and yet the idea of getting the Belgians to change from Englebert to something like US Rubber Belgium was clearly absurd.

US Rubber and its consultants, Lippincott & Margulies of New York and London, had to weigh up the very real advantages of what would have to be an entirely new corporate name used right across the world—the advantages of product rationalisation, marketing, supply and advertising—with the disadvantages resulting from the disappearance of each existing and well established company name, including that of US Rubber itself.

Eventually Lippincott & Margulies produced an umbrella name, a kind of surname, which was used for a time in conjunction with all of the company names and brand names. The name chosen was Uniroyal. It was based, they claim, on a combination of Uni, as in United States (or one might add, perhaps unfairly, Unilever, Unigate, Uniflex, Univac and a few more) and Royal from the well known tyre brand name. Uniroyal was not perhaps the most inspiring of names, but it was adequate.

Some of the companies that went to form Uniroyal

After a relatively short time, just a couple of years, all the old individual company names were phased out and Uniroyal replaced them. For the first time, Uniroyal was able to launch international campaigns to introduce international products. Its growth since then has been quite remarkable. US Rubber, Englebert and the rest have simply sunk without trace.

Some name changes cannot really be regarded as an improvement. They only make sense in an organisation chart. On 1 June 1976 a company called GM Power Products-Europe became known as Detroit Diesel Allison International-Europe. This is the advertisement that appeared to announce the event. It is amusing to think that an organisation as big as GM can show such ineptitude in at least some of its outposts. Other name changes make good marketing sense—few could make worse!

JUNE 1

TODAY, WE'RE GOING TO MAKE A NAME FOR OURSELVES.

A new name, from June 1st this year GM POWER PRODUCTS—EUROPE will be known as:
DETROIT DIESEL ALLISON INTERNATIONAL—EUROPE

We feel that this new name is more descriptive of our activities in the diesel and transmission fields.

Our Detroit and Bedford Diesels and Allison Transmissions are in use worldwide, in public works and civil engineering, road transport, marine and electrical power generation.

A unique chain of specialised distributors and dealers back every sale with an unrivalled servicing organisation—world wide.

Don't forget—new name—same reliable service.

*Detroit Diesel Allison International—Europe, Wellingborough, Northants, England.

Detroit Diesel Allison International-Europe

It's a powerful name

Aspro Nicholas, an Australian based company, founded its fortunes on Aspro, a heavily advertised aspirin-based product. For a variety of reasons, according to James Pilditch, chairman of Allied International Designers, a well known British-based design consultancy company, the Aspro Nicholas people wanted to adopt what he calls 'a broad scientific profile'. In other words, in terms of product and corporate style they were going up the market. Quite reasonably, AID proposed that the continued use of Aspro in the group name would hinder the development of the classier image. Aspro Nicholas changed its name to Nicholas Products. They still make and sell Aspro but now it is perceived as what it is, just one of a range of products.

One of the industries that has seen the most dramatic name changes in the last few years is aerospace. In Britain when the merger between Bristol, Vickers, English Electric, Hunting and Percival took place a new name became essential. With staggering originality somebody turned up with, wait for it, the British Aircraft Corporation. What didn't go into BAC went to form Hawker Siddeley. Now that Hawker and BAC have been nationalised, the new name that has been coined 'temporarily' is British Aerospace.

When BAC was formed it was essential to get the 'one family' feeling as quickly as possible, and no doubt the new

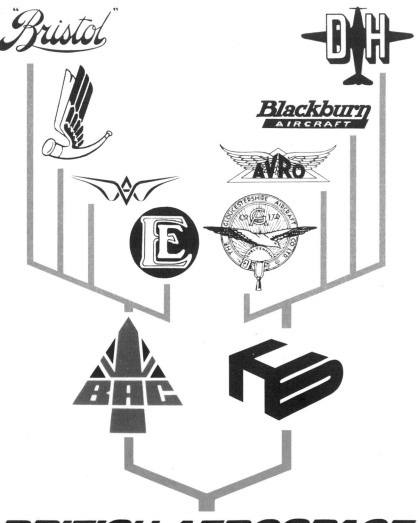

name, however banal and predictable, helped to do that. What also helped BAC was that its products, or brands if you prefer—the One Eleven, Jet Provost, Lightning and of course Concorde, and the Tornado (formerly MRCA) in which it is a co-producer—are much better known than the company, so that continuity was assured.

The units within Aerospatiale, or as it sometimes confusingly calls itself, SNIAS, which constitutes the major portion of the French airframe industry, have been renamed not once but twice, and in some cases more. As successive waves of rationalisation overtook them, all the old names disappeared. So effectively have they been superseded that it requires an aircraft historian to go much further back than Sud & Nord Aviation, which lie in their immediate past.

The old Bleriot factory in Paris is now incongruously a part of Aerospatiale

The reasons for the new name reflect a series of political decisions involving the regrouping and redeployment of the French aircraft industry. Name changes were imperative if the corporate objectives were to be achieved.

One of the most valuable, and certainly one of the best known, names in the engineering world is Rolls-Royce, which is still a synonym for the best there is. It is redolent of Edwardian glamour, of the Honourable Charles Rolls, who was killed in an air crash at Bournemouth in 1910, and the British engineering genius of Henry Royce, the dour, bearded perfectionist who worked himself to death.

Nowadays there are two Rolls-Royce companies: Rolls-Royce Motors, which makes cars, diesel engines and light aircraft engines; and Rolls-Royce Ltd, builder of the jet engines of many civil and military aircraft.

The history of Rolls-Royce in aero engines, so far from being a stately progress from one triumph to the next, has been turbulent and occasionally disastrous. Over the years, however, it has managed, sometimes only just, to absorb virtually all of its old rivals, including companies with traditions and history as rich as Rolls-Royce itself.

By the middle 1960s there were only two major aircraft engine companies left in Britain—Rolls-Royce and Bristol Siddeley. Bristol Siddeley was no sickly weakling; on the contrary, in many ways it was in a much better state than Rolls-Royce. Its technology was very advanced, it had some prestigious contracts, and it had a healthy, long-standing dislike of its arrogant competitor.

Bristol Siddeley was a merged company. It was based on the old Bristol engine company, Armstrong Siddeley Motors of Coventry, and the much smaller de Havilland and Blackburn engine companies. Although it was in good shape it couldn't compare with Rolls-Royce in terms of international reputation. When the decision to merge Rolls-Royce with Bristol Siddeley was taken—and this was of course also a political decision—naturally somebody had to decide what the new merged company should be called. Bristol Siddeley, which had been rapidly building up its own name and reputation, was faced with the inevitable. Even though it was a merger of equal partners, the name of the new company was to be Rolls-Royce.

Now Rolls-Royce, as anyone who has dealt with the company knows, has many virtues, but it has never been strong on tact or humility. When the decision to call the merged company Rolls-Royce was taken, it went almost without saying that Rolls-Royce rubbed Bristol Siddeley's nose in it. Rolls-Royce executives were not slow to claim that they had once again galloped to the rescue of an ailing company. They were also eager to offer unsolicited technical advice to their erstwhile competitors.

The change of name, and more particularly the way it was handled, caused bitter resentment inside Bristol Siddeley which would in the normal course of events have taken years to die. Then a totally unexpected event took place: Rolls-Royce went bankrupt in the most public and humiliating fashion; it was a kind of classical Greek hubris. This disaster had absolutely nothing to do with the Bristol Siddeley merger; it was related to the Lockheed Tristar contract, which the old Rolls-Royce had negotiated some years before. But the whole of Rolls-Royce was disgraced and the Bristol Siddeley people were in it up to their necks with the old Rolls-Royce people.

Eventually the British government stepped in; the motor car activities were hived off, the aircraft engine activities were nationalised, and Rolls-Royce Ltd is now a state-owned company. Time is slowly healing the wounds, but the Rolls-Royce/Bristol Siddeley story remains a classic of how not to do it. It wasn't that what was done was so wrong, but that the way it was done was so unfortunate.

In a less contentious field, Mitchell Cotts, the international transport and engineering group, bought a miscellaneous collection of air freight companies a few years ago. In Britain these companies were called Wisk, in South Africa Miller Weedon, and in Australia Corrigans. Some of the companies were well known nationally, and some were involved in businesses other than air freight. After discussions and consultations it was decided to call the whole lot Mitchell Cotts Airfreight and give it a powerful new identity. The operation was quick and successful; Mitchell Cotts became established as an air freight name with no difficulty. No clients were lost and the resultant gain from using one name and one style all over the world was immediate and quantifiable.

There are plenty of precedents for name changes. Most companies recognise when a name change is called for, but are generally very hesitant to take the plunge.

When a company wants to change its name it has a number of different sorts of name to choose from. Terence Griffin has worked out that there are six different name categories. The first is the name of an individual or individuals, usually the company's founder. Ford, Philips, Lucas, Dassault, Marks & Spencer and Krupp are all examples in this category. Although many companies start with the founder's name it is very rare for a company to make a name change to that of an individual.

Second come descriptive names. These usually describe the company's activity and often have some geographical qualifications. Yorkshire Imperial Metals, Badische Anilin- & Soda-Fabrik, Occidental Oil, English China Clays, General Motors and Union Deutsche Lebensmittelwerke all fall into this category. Most companies thinking of changing their names examine descriptive names very closely since it is the most obvious field in which to search. When, for example, the sickly Hudson and Nash car companies amalgamated in the 1950s they became American Motors.

When Heinkel, Focke-Wulf, Weserflug and the other German aircraft companies joined forces they became Vereinigte Flugtechnische Werke (United Aircraft Works).

When the container consortium was formed between Europe and North America, incorporating Cunard, Holland-America and the Compagnie Générale Transatlantique it was called Atlantic Container Line.

This category has a lot of potential disadvantages, of which the main one is that what starts out by being an accurate description can very soon get out of date. The name Baden Aniline and Soda Works, which is the English translation of the full name of BASF, has little relevance to the company's current activities or geographical locations and is almost comically anachronistic. Both the Imperial Tobacco Company, which now calls itself the Imperial Group, and British American Tobacco (BAT) are examples of companies that have outgrown their descriptions. And of course US Rubber, British Ropes and Jute Industries, all of which as we have already seen changed their names because of their limitations, come into this category. The only names that always remain appropriate are so vague—General Motors, General Mills, General Foods—that they start off not meaning much. Also in this category fall words like European and Electronics, which drift in and out of fashion. Despite its superficial attractions this category has a number of disadvantages.

The third category, abbreviated names, are familiar versions of a larger name—names like PanAm, Conoco, Preussag. There is quite a lot to be said for abbreviated names: they are short, easy to use, and can be invested with some kind of relevance, and yet they are not as restrictive as fully descriptive names. There are not many people who would have associated the old Socony company with Standard Oil of New York, or for that matter Esso with Standard Oil of New Jersey, but the rationale was there for anybody who wanted it. The abbreviated name category should be examined carefully by those companies looking for a change.

The fourth group are initials. Initials need much heavier promotion than other names in order to break through the barrier of anonymity which they themselves create; they must be used so regularly that they become more familiar than the full name. Sometimes this happens: KLM is an example. Not many people inside the Netherlands, and practically nobody outside it, says Koninklijke Luchvaart Maatschappij in the course of conversation. Svenska Kullagerfabriken, the Swedish ballbearing company, fortunately for those of us who don't speak Swedish, initialled itself into SKF years ago.

The trouble with initials is not only that they start anonymous, but that they also quite often stay that way. It is true that IBM, ICI, BP are all quite clear and meaningful, but what about BSC? Is it British Sugar Corporation or British Shoe Corporation, or British Steel Corporation or what?

Initials can also mean different things in different places. Brown Boveri, the Swiss engineering group, calls itself BBC throughout Europe, but not in Britain, for obvious reasons.

The fifth category consists of names like Kodak, Shell or Viyella. These have usually been coined in the way that Eastman invented Kodak which he thought sounded like the click of a camera shutter. He could have called it the American Photographic Company. If he had, we would probably call Kodak APC, or maybe Apco, today.

Some abstract names once had a meaning which soon became irrelevant. Shell is an example of this. The origins of the name Shell are quite interesting. Most people who work for Shell don't seem to be aware of them. Robert Henriques, the biographer of Marcus Samuel who founded the British half of the company from which the name derives, refers in *Marcus Samuel—First Viscount Bearsted, Founder of 'Shell' Transport and Trading Company* to an incident that he considers unreliably reported in a book called *The Black Golconda* by Isaac F Marcosson.

Marcosson tells the story like this: 'One day the Samuel children went to Margate on a holiday. Romping on the beach they saw their first shells. They carried a modest lunch in a small box. When the food had been disposed of they amused themselves by fastening shells on the empty box. They were so pleased with their handiwork that they brought it home and showed it to their parents. It gave the elder Samuel an idea . . .'

Henriques then takes up the story: 'Certainly that popular Victorian knick-knack, the box, needle-case, pin-cushion, blotter, or photograph-frame, ornamented with shells and known generically as "the shell-box", became an important item of trade for the Samuels, so that ultimately they employed several designers and shell cleaners and some forty girls in the manufacture of these delights. Their speciality was the souvenir inscribed "A Gift from Brighton" and from all the other popular seaside resorts. Certainly, also, when the younger Marcus wanted a trade name for the oil he sold, names for the ships which he built to carry it and ultimately a name for the company he formed, he got all those names from this department of his father's business.'

In fact, the company that Marcus Samuel launched to trade with the Far East was originally called Samuel Samuel & Co. It wasn't called Shell until some years after its foundation. It's possible that if Marcus Samuel had not changed his mind we would nowadays be talking about SamSam or maybe Samsam rather than Shell.

Shell, which apparently acquired its name in a casual and haphazard fashion, is a classic in the abstract name field. The word shell is now synonymous with the oil company, but 'shell' also means high explosives and sea shells in at least one language, and it may well have different meanings in others.

Of course abstract names need to be put into a context before they can work effectively, but as the Shell example shows they do not need to be intrinsically anonymous.

The sixth and final category of names that Terence Griffin describes are what he calls 'analogous' names. The Sunlight Laundry, The Crow Carrying Company, Quaker Foods—all these names try to draw an analogy between the company and a specific object or quality. Quaker is a synonym, at least in the English language, for integrity and solid worth, hence Quaker Foods. Sunlight implies bright, shining and sparkling, hence Sunlight Laundry. Volvo is taken from the Latin 'I roll'—possibly the analogy is a little far-fetched here, bearing in mind that Latin is not very widely used in the latter part of the twentieth century. This kind of name is generally used much more for brands than for companies. It is easy to see the advantages of such names: they are striking, individual and they clearly project a picture of the company they describe. On the other hand they have the disadvantages that they rarely work in more than one or two languages and they can become inappropriate in time.

There is no subject that is more emotional and less susceptible to rational analysis than a name. It requires a major exercise of imagination to visualise what a company would look and feel like if its name were changed. All the possible new names appear strange, irrelevant and arbitrary because until they are actually in use they are simply exercises in imagination, or lack of it.

Consider your own name. Can you imagine being called anything else? But most women who marry take their husband's name without appearing to suffer major inconvenience, let alone disaster. Those of us who have been through the exercise of naming children will recall how difficult it is to make the choice in the first place, and yet once the choice is made, how rapidly it gains momentum and therefore weight and credibility. It always seems to suit the child particularly well, and in retrospect usually appears to have been the only possible decision.

Exactly the same thing happens when a company makes a choice. Provided that it makes its choice on clear criteria, picks a name that is appropriate and promotes it with enthusiasm, then the name will fit the company and seem apt and relevant.

It is possible to produce a set of criteria to help an organisation to pick a name. The relative significance of the criteria varies of course: a company operating in 128 countries with 14 major product groups will have different preoccupations from one operating only in Germany in, say, the steel stockholding business, or from a new borough in London incorporating three smaller units. These criteria cannot be looked at baldly; some kind of weighting must be given according to the circumstances in which the organisation finds itself.

The criteria for a name are:
It should be easy to read
It should be easy to pronounce, preferably in any language
It should have no disagreeable associations, preferably in any language
It should be suitable for use if the organisation expands into different activities
It should be registerable, or at least protectable
It should not date

It should, if possible, relate to the activity of the company
It should be idiosyncratic
It should be something with which a powerful visual style
can be associated
It should have charisma

I once discussed this set of criteria with a client, and he complained that, bearing in mind that we didn't want initials and couldn't use the name of an individual or a geographical or activity description, all the best names had gone—they had been used up by everyone else!

That's a bit like complaining that family names should only be used once. I have a cousin called Wally Olins, but I don't mind, and so far as I know he doesn't either. We don't look the same, and we aren't in the same business. Although our names are the same we have different identities.

The same rule applies amongst corporations. Obviously nobody wants to use conflicting initials if it can be avoided, but names can come to mean a whole series of different things in appropriate visual settings.

Take Lincoln, for instance. (If you haven't cheated and looked over the page at the illustrations), ask yourself what Lincoln stands for. It can be a President, a make of car, a city, a colour, a biscuit, a cathedral, pipe tobacco and a large number of other things, depending on the visual and the verbal context.

Similarly Avon can be cosmetics, a river, a jet engine and a rubber company. Nobody confuses any of them because the contexts in which they operate are so different.

Returning to Shell for a moment, no consultant today would recommend to a company concerned with the exploration, refining and distribution of highly volatile fluids, gases and chemical compounds that it should call itself by the same name as a highly explosive projectile, but since in Marcus Samuel's day there were no consultants, and he wasn't too bothered, the Shell Company casually acquired its name. The chances are, despite its own obsession with conchology, that most of its customers, who after all don't speak English, don't even know that the symbol and the name represent the same thing.

Of course while it's certainly true that names are important, and it is difficult to carry on life as Hindustan Tea Estates when you are in the international heavy haulage business, we shouldn't exaggerate the problems. After all, if Hoechst can get away with its name, which no non-German speaker can pronounce, then most people needn't worry too much.

The fascinating thing about names is that, like all revolutions, they are the cause of much trouble and emotional ferment before the decision, but once the whole affair is over the problems are completely forgotten.

Chapter 12
The design consultants
How graphic designers turned into multi-disciplinary consultants.

In 1907 Peter Behrens, one of Germany's leading modern architects then aged 39, was appointed by Herr Jordan of the AEG, Allgemeine Elektricitäts-Gesellschaft, to be its corporate architect and design consultant. AEG, which under Walter Rathenau had become one of Germany's leading electrical companies, wanted Behrens to look at all aspects of its visual output. He was not only to design factories and offices but products too. He was to be responsible for the quality of everything that could affect the visual image of AEG.

Sir Nikolaus Pevsner in *Pioneers of Modern Design* describes in detail Behrens' Berlin turbine factory of 1909, which he says was 'perhaps the most beautiful industrial building ever created up to that time'. Pevsner goes on:

'While Behrens was employed on such monumental tasks, he managed to spend the same amount of care and thought on improvements in the design of small things for everyday use and larger things of so utilitarian a kind that they had never before been regarded as works of art at all.'

Pevsner is here referring to Behrens' work on diverse kinds of electrical equipment.

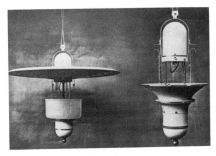

AEG, 1909—an early modern corporate identity

Among those working in Behrens' office while he was engaged in these pioneer efforts in design consultancy was Walter Gropius. Gropius left Behrens in 1911 and after carrying out some work on his own went on to start the Bauhaus, which has probably been the greatest single influence on design in the twentieth century.

Although the Bauhaus was widely known and indeed extremely controversial in its day, its direct influence on industrial concerns was small. There were very few industrialists who used industrial design or even knew what it was. Milner Gray, one of the great pioneers of British design consultancy, recalls the atmosphere of the 1930s very clearly. He says that for most of his working life design consultancy has been seeking recognition as a separate and significant business function.

Before the Second World War the number of corporate design schemes carried out in Britain through professional designers could be counted on the fingers of one hand and things weren't much different in any other country. Whenever a major scheme was carried out, however, it was publicised almost endlessly and this gave the impression that much more was going on than was actually the case. Although there were a few professional designers and design companies many of these, even in the United States, found it hard to make a living.

They did all sorts of things: they worked on interior design, graphics and product design. Where they were used by big business, which wasn't often, the businessmen who used them were also design patrons. The Anderson family of the Orient Line and Frank Pick of London Transport were typical British examples. These men were enthusiasts; no orthodox businessman would have used professional design or designers in the 1930s, it just wasn't seriously considered. Milner Gray remembers a British managing director saying to him at this time, 'I used a designer once. Thirty shillings a week down the drain.'

The mainstream of designers, which perhaps could be more accurately described as a main trickle, transferred from Germany to the United States in the 1930s. They were principally concerned with the design of products: Raymond Loewy, originally an illustrator, first became famous for his work on railway trains and then on automobiles. Another famous designer of the day was Norman Bel Geddes who worked on equipment for IBM, the young Eliot Noyes worked with him.

These men and their contemporaries were concerned with what the product looked like and how it worked. They were deeply involved in discussions about form and function. Debates centred around the phrase 'if it looks right, it is right'. These discussions have as much relevance to today's problems as Victorian arguments on whether photography is an art form.

Inevitably it was only a relatively short step from working on the design of products to looking at the environment in which they were found. From products and showrooms there was a natural progression to graphics. Designers had worked on publicity brochures, posters and other printed matter for many years and it was really only a question of bringing it all together into one package.

Jay Doblin, one of the most serious of the veteran design thinkers, who started designing streamlined trains back in the 1930s with Loewy recalls that the first major intentional corporate identity was carried out for International Harvester in the early 1940s.

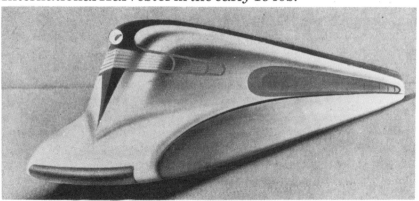

Loewy's 'Fast Commuter' train, 1930s

Organisations like International Harvester and IBM in the United States, Olivetti in Italy and London Transport in Britain got involved in unified design programmes for a number of reasons. Of course they appreciated the benefits that unified design and a distinctive house style would bring in terms of internal morale, public recognition, higher standards of performance, improved recruitment and so on, but the individual executives who commissioned the design programmes were also convinced that what they were doing would put them on the side of the angels. Good design meant doing good, raising visual standards everywhere, making the environment more agreeable.

There is an inescapable similarity between Adriano Olivetti, the prince-patron of all that is best in modern Italian design, and Lorenzo de Medici, the patron of the Florentine masters of the Renaissance.

It is difficult to judge when the climate began to change. It varied from country to country and it was affected both by the very rapid growth of international business, which intuitively looked for some kind of design instrument to provide cohesion, and also by a very few design consultants who realised they had something else to sell in addition to that unquantifiable factor 'good design'.

The main thrust for the development of corporate identity programmes came from the United States. The practical and business-like designers in the US, seeing openings in packaging, symbol design, interiors, and product design, moved from small and sometimes isolated bases into major corporate identity programmes. Not only were graphic designers more business-like in the US; businessmen like Walter Paepcke of the Container Corporation of America and Tom Watson Jnr of IBM were also more imaginative. The IBM operation in which Tom Watson Jnr, chief executive of the company, worked with Eliot Noyes to improve all design produced by the company was not new; after all, AEG had been working with Behrens in Germany as far back as 1907. What was different was that, as IBM's example was seen to work in terms of sales, recruitment, image and prestige, other large American companies followed it.

A few design consultants, and once again the pioneer developments were in the United States, began to appreciate that some of their very large clients were afflicted with communication problems that graphic design alone could not solve. Companies with different names in different places, companies changing the nature of their activities, companies merging, companies acquiring—all of these needed investigation, analysis and recommendations that were different from anything that designers had previously been able to provide.

This led some design consultancy companies to widen the scope of their activities. They began to take their first tentative and hesitant steps towards broader consultancy. For the first time some American design consultants began to talk to the wider world of American business in a language it could understand—the language of dollars and cents. Naturally they needed to wrap it up a bit and to put it into acceptable jargon, so American design consultants— or as they now began to call themselves, consultants in design, communication and marketing—started talking about global marketing and stock market prices.

This change in emphasis enabled the design consultants to tackle the massive heartland of American business, where dedicated patrons of design were pretty thin on the ground. It was at this point that industry's attitude to design began to change. It was no longer a minor, interesting, but for the most part irrelevant, art form, but a significant tool of business.

The archetype, or as it claims the prototype, of the new type of design consultants is Lippincott & Margulies of New York and London. Lippincott & Margulies does not sell design; it sells business concepts that involve a number of skills of which design is one. It talks a lot about corporate communications, about marketing, about the use of design in creating an appropriate industrial and commercial environment for solving special business problems. It knows that most American businessmen are sensitive to the stock market price and so it talks a lot about that too.

Lippincott & Margulies spawned a whole series of children. Many of the major exponents of this type of consultancy operation are in some way modelled on the Lippincott & Margulies company.

Inevitably the new kind of design consultancy employs people with a much wider variety of skills than the more traditional type of operation. Many of the executives in the new generation of consultancy companies are not designers at all; they are ex-advertising copywriters or marketing men with a background in consumer products. Quite often the design consultancies recruit people from other parts of the consulting world, from the major management consultants like McKinsey or Booz Allen Hamilton, or from public relations companies.

At the same time the attitude of the graphic designers themselves has changed somewhat. Under the influence of the Bauhaus and the holier than thou attitudes of the 1930s and 1940s, graphic designers kept themselves apart from advertising people, although both groups were engaged in problems of visual communication.

The purist typographers with their roots in the Swiss school were contemptuous of the commercialism and lack of rigour displayed by advertising agencies, while the agencies regarded the classical graphic designers as an irrelevance. In the 1950s and 1960s some graphic designers began tentatively to move between the two worlds. Much more important, the two groups of people began to influence each other.

At first the relationship between the advertising agencies and the new design companies was ambivalent. Initially many advertising agencies saw corporate identity, packaging and other graphic design specialities as something their own 'collateral' or 'below the line' departments could readily handle either for a small fee or, if the account was big enough, free. However, on the basis, to use the time-honoured phrase, that if you pay peanuts you get monkeys, not many clients were satisfied with the results. Another agency reaction, no doubt deriving from their temperamental insecurity, was that the design consultant was somehow a threat. Design consultancies were, it was thought, a new kind of organisation aimed at stealing agency business or reducing their influence. The third agency reaction was that the design consultancies were simply grandiose art studios with an inflated idea of their own significance. All these ideas are now dead or dying and for the most part far-sighted advertising agencies encourage their clients to use design consultants where appropriate.

The growth of consultancies that exist to deal with a series of complex corporate organisational problems using design as a tool, has of course not taken place without much heart searching, nor has their progress been unchallenged. It is said by their critics, many of whom are other designers, that consultancy companies of this kind rarely produce good design work. They are accused of having an internal climate that is inimical to real creativity, of under-estimating the significance of design in the solution of the problem, and of pandering to the client's desire for orthodoxy and reassurance. It's true that there is a deadly sameness about many of the solutions produced by consultancy companies of this type. It's equally true though that many of the other design consultants, the ones who reject all the modern paraphernalia, also often produce conventional and unimaginative solutions.

Another complaint that traditional design consultants make about the more broad-based companies is that they employ production line techniques; they walk in, do the job and walk out, all within a year or two. The traditional consultants, some of whom spend many years with their clients, say that this superficial face lifting is useless and even counter-productive. The consultancy companies in the newer tradition say that most of their clients, who are not after all design patrons, simply won't pay to have them around for very long, and that although they would all love to do a deep and thorough job, nobody wants to starve.

Behind this squabbling lies a profound issue. Traditionally designers—not just graphic designers, but all kinds of designers—have believed that the interests of industry are inimical to those of design. This feeling has been actively fostered in some art schools. Even when there is no overt prejudice against business and businessmen, the art student has rarely been given serious commercial, industrial or management training.

For their part, businessmen have generally tended to regard anything to do with creativity, art or design either as something to do with women or as a process that is mysterious and terrifying—or both.

In order to make plain their feelings of mutual suspicion, or even antipathy, businessmen and designers have put out appropriate signals. They have worn different clothes, eaten at different places and lived in different districts. Designers have caricatured businessmen as coarse, vulgar philistines, prepared to do anything for money. Businessmen have thought of designers as effete, impractical, idealistic and probably politically and emotionally unreliable.

These grotesque caricatures are at the root of the difficulties through which the world of design consultancy is currently moving. Some traditional designers, many of them very young people, are having difficulty in coming to terms with the idea that design and business are not necessarily antipathetic and fundamentally hostile.

Corporate identity is at the centre of this debate. Everything in design terms springs from the identity of the company—its architecture, its packaging, its publicity programmes—but it is manifestly impossible for a graphic designer by himself to comprehend clearly the nature of an organisation's identity. Too many cultural, organisational, political and psychological factors are involved for which the designer has no training.

The problems of corporate identity are often expressed in simplistic terms by the industrialist. He thinks he needs a corporate symbol to pull everything together, so he goes to a graphic designer who either provides a corporate symbol that is entirely useless or who appreciates the profound and complex nature of the problem and calls in a group of colleagues with different backgrounds and disciplines to help him resolve the problem.

The plain fact is that graphic designers working by themselves are rarely able to resolve corporate identity problems of any real complexity. The argument for the multidisciplinary design consultancy with its designers, marketing men, psychologists, sociologists and economists is unassailable.

In practice nowadays the design consultancy scene can be loosely divided into three streams, which I have called the design Masters, the Professionals and the Rest.

The Masters are made up of individual designers or design groups with a distinguished national or international reputation. Designers of this eminence can for the most part pick and choose their work and can afford to be fastidious about what they do and who they do it for. Their attitude to their work and their creative style is always singular and often idiosyncratic and there is no such thing as a typical design Master.

Often the Masters tend to prize the long-standing and close relationships they have with their clients. They tend to be on close terms with, or at least have good access to, the chief executives of the organisations with which they deal, and the chief executives normally make their commitment to long-term design programmes very clear. All this of course is conducive to the development of an atmosphere that allows good design to flourish.

The companies who use design Masters have respect for design. Often the design programme—for example in the cases of IBM, Mobil and Olivetti, three companies who use Masters for their design work—is seen to be part of a long-term effort on the part of the company to communicate clearly and openly with all of its audiences. Both IBM and Mobil have expressed particular and public concern about the image of big business and they use design in the broadest sense to project an identity that is favourable and which they apparently believe to be accurate.

Design Masters flourish in the United States and in every major country in Europe. They tend to run very small organisations, in which the Master himself usually practises with a few acolytes. For the most part, for reasons which I have explained, the Masters do not get involved with complex corporate identity programmes, although one or two of them have spent their entire working lives with just a few companies. For them, the late Eliot Noyes can speak. Noyes worked for IBM, Mobil, Westinghouse and PanAm. His relations with most of his clients were close, personal and long lasting. He was regarded as being primarily responsible for the success of the IBM programme with which he was associated since the 1940s until his death in 1977. Noyes was one of the most respected and successful consultants in the world and his views are well worth airing.

In a discussion I had with him in 1976 he made it plain that the act of creating a corporate image as though it were a piece of cake or other merchandise was revolting to him. The IBM programme was not consciously created in this way at all: Noyes was working for Norman Bel Geddes and was given the job of designing a typewriter for IBM. During the course of this job he met Tom Watson Jnr of IBM. Then the Geddes firm was dissolved and he was asked to finish off the design, and in 1948 or so he was asked to do other things for them. He started redesigning office floors and cafeterias and showrooms. He tried to persuade IBM that their showroom on 57th Street, New York, which was all plush carpets and gold pelmets with IBM machines sitting about in it, was inappropriate; there was no hint that they produced the most advanced electronic machines in the world. Noyes took a long time to persuade Watson to move; he even handed him some Olivetti publicity material to show him what other people were doing. According to Noyes the whole thing grew slowly. Noyes kept on saying that everything looked a mess—the buildings, the equipment, the publicity material, the trademarks. He tried to persuade Watson to do something about it, to make it look better. Watson was eventually won over and agreed that something should be done.

At that time, according to Noyes, in the early 1950s, although the notion of a corporate identity programme was known theoretically, it had never been carried out. Here there seems to be some conflict with Doblin's view that the International Harvester programme predates these events. Noyes was convinced from the beginning that an overall design programme with one designer doing everything was nonsense, but he knew that a group of consultants could do a great deal for IBM. First he brought in Paul Rand to work on graphics and then a wide range of other designers joined from all over the world.

Interestingly, Noyes carried out no analysis of the company. Perhaps he didn't need to since he did after all know it well. He said that the programme was based simply on the idea that IBM was a modern company producing modern products and that was what it ought to look like. The design programme, Noyes felt, expressed IBM's consistency of quality. It is now part of IBM's way of life, part of what IBM is.

It all sounds simple and easy and in a way it is. Noyes felt that there were four principles essential to successful corporate design. First, the design consultant needs a close personal relationship with the chief executive. Second, the programme starts at the part that really needs doing and that is really important (such as petrol stations for Mobil, or office machines for IBM). Third, the consultant appoints other designers, architects, graphic designers and product designers for whom he has a real respect and then he lets them get on with it. Fourth, the relationship must be an enduring one.

Now, although these precepts are admirable, and the results are excellent, there aren't many IBMs and Mobils around. Nor are there many design consultants who would be content to live with only a very few companies during their entire working lives. Although the Masters are very significant and are rightly (in some ways) much praised, in their attitudes, in their relationships with their clients and therefore in the atmosphere in which they operate they are wholly atypical.

The second group of design consultants are those I have called the Professionals. Like the Masters, the Professionals as a group are rather difficult to describe; each company tends to be different in personality, in experience and in its bias. Although the influence of Walter Margulies and of the Lippincott & Margulies company has, as I have indicated, been very significant, his hard selling and jargon-ridden style has not been followed by everyone.

For the most part the Professionals exist in the United States and Great Britain, although there are also a few companies of this kind developing in Europe and particularly in Holland. They consist of companies of between, say, 20 and 60 people whose principal characteristic is that the people in them come from widely differing backgrounds and professional disciplines. One company of this kind, for example, might contain among its senior members architects, graphic designers, marketing men, economists, generalist consultants and sociologists. This mixture of talents, skills and experience will determine the way in which the design consultancy goes after its work, the way in which it carries it out and the way in which it projects itself.

Professional design consultants of this type face many problems. They are trying to find a way of describing what they do so that it is clear and simple and doesn't seem to have too much bias towards design—a word which is loose and open to considerable misinterpretation. They often describe themselves as consultants in design, marketing and communications. They sometimes spend time and money in justifying their activities to their clients.

These professional design consultancy companies want to position themselves somewhere between a management consultancy, an architectural practice, a PR operation and an advertising agency. They are groping towards a position in which they can say to their clients that they deal with corporate problems that are resolved, partially at any rate, through the medium of design.

They appreciate that industry demands from its suppliers certain patterns of behaviour and structure to which they must conform. They see the world of business and industry opening up before them and they are anxious not to miss the opportunities this brings.

On the other hand, they recognise that the posture they need to adopt in order to seize these opportunities may lead them into a situation in which their originality, objectivity, enthusiasm and creativity are diminished. This is their dilemma.

On balance it is the professional design consultants who are now making the most effective contribution towards integrating design into the management structure.

It is perhaps this concern about their loss of integrity and professionalism as designers, and the need to associate with marketing men, sociologists, economists, psychologists and accountants in some wider grouping, that has delayed the development of professional design consultancy companies in the major European countries. Even in Britain and the USA their numbers are quite small: there are perhaps 20 to 30 professional design consultancy companies in the United States, each employing between 20 and 60 people.

Most of the Professionals are located in New York and many have in one way or another sprung from the loins of Lippincott & Margulies. Naturally the largest design consultancy in the world is in the United States. This is Landor Associates, which is agreeably located on a ferry boat in San Francisco. About half its work comes from US sources, the rest comes from Western Europe, South America and Japan.

Another group of Professionals is based in Chicago which is the home of Ralph Eckerstrom's Unimark. Unimark made a brave, pioneering and for a short time successful attempt to set up a chain of design consultancy companies around the world. In the event it didn't quite come off, but it almost did.

In Britain there are about 10 Professionals—that is companies employing more than 20 people offering, or purporting to offer, a wide range of design and communication services. Some of the British companies are active in Europe and the Middle East. Although the Americans have come to Europe and have had some modest success, no European Professionals have been successful in the United States so far.

The method of work of professional design consultants on both sides of the Atlantic is much the same. For the most part they do not enjoy the close and enduring relationship with their clients described by Eliot Noyes; they operate in a less sympathetic environment. They have to attune their behaviour to that of other consultants. They deal with clients who seek reassurance in formalised systems and research back-up, so they react accordingly.

Some of the Professionals use formal research systems a great deal, some only a little. In some cases they have close and effective relationships with the top men amongst their clients, in other cases they deal either with the marketing or PR people. In general their relationships with a company last a relatively short time—say between six months and four years.

The influence of the Masters and the Professionals is absurdly disproportionate to their total numbers. It is worth remembering that the vast proportion of designers—graphic, interior or product—work in small groups of two or three people and are for the most part unaffected by and ignorant of the somewhat rarefied stance affected by the Masters and the commercial pioneering and soul-searching of the Professionals. This third stream, whom we might perhaps unfairly call the Rest, are the bulk of the designers who hammer up their shingle in Lyons or Manchester or Düsseldorf or Bologna or Boston.

All over the world there are independent designers working on designs for restaurants, house styles for local banks, corporate identities and packaging designs for supermarket chains. The one stunning thing about their work is that there is so much of it. In quantity it must outnumber the work of all the other designers by a hundred to one. It is the work of these people that gives the world much of its visual style. They have small budgets, they don't get too involved with conceptualising, their clients are not necessarily very sophisticated—although some of them may be—and they just get on with the job.

It is perhaps wrong to give so little emphasis to the work created by the Rest and so much to that done by the Professionals and the Masters. Much of the work produced both by the Masters and the Professionals is self-conscious. It frequently panders to the built-in desire of all huge companies to look cool, distant, omnipotent and omniscient—in some curious way above the battle. Many good intuitive graphic designers with uncluttered minds can still produce original and exciting work in powerful local or national traditions. On the other hand a lot of the design work produced by small, independent freelance designers is clearly not so much traditional as derivative.

Summing up then, the present state of the art is relatively undeveloped. Designers with their various tortuous historical traditions are tentatively, or in some cases enthusiastically, embracing management sciences; they are attempting to build bridges with business schools and to jockey for position with older and perhaps more clearly understood consultants for the right and privilege of teaching big business how to suck eggs.

Like most consultants, the design consultants and the corporate identity specialists—not necessarily the same thing—contain among them some genuinely gifted people, as well as a few shysters and con-men (although not very many because there are easier ways of making a living) and a great many bewildered, honest designers who don't quite realise what has hit them and still confuse themselves and their clients with the notion that symbols, logos and other graphic impedimenta make up corporate identity.

Because the business is in its childhood, if not its infancy, any guesses about its long-term direction are likely to be about as accurate as predictions about the personality, character and career prospects of a five-year-old child. Nevertheless it appears that there are certain clear lines of probable development.

The corporate identity business will in one sense become more like a boardroom consultancy business. It will have a level of consultants with different disciplines and skills—say architects, economists, accountants, psychologists and sociologists—who will be able to work with a company and to advise it on all of those matters to which this book refers.

At another and equal level, the design consultancy business will be able to implement its recommendations. These will not simply be related to graphics, but to products, architecture, packaging, and to all other appropriate manifestations of the organisation.

Within design consultancies, graphic designers will inevitably lose their pre-eminence as people from other and complementary disciplines emerge. I see architects, product designers and environmental designers being of equal significance with graphic designers in consultancy companies, together with consultants, whose background may be in anthropology, sociology, economics, marketing and other 'non-design' subjects.

As to size, experience clearly indicates that beyond a given point it is difficult for companies involved in creative thinking to function at their best. Of course there are architectural firms and advertising agencies and engineering consultancies with hundreds and even a few with thousands of people in tens of branches and some of these produce excellent work. However, experiences of large size design consultancies have so far been most unfortunate: only one company in the United States tried to get very big very fast; it succeeded for a short time but it got smaller even faster. I incline to the view that despite many pressures to expand most corporate identity consultancies will not be bigger than about 100 people.

I cannot see the vacuum that currently exists in Europe, with the exception of Britain, remaining unfilled indefinitely or for that matter even for long. I would expect to see a rapid development of design consultancies based on the US/British model in France and more particularly in Germany. The individual skills exist; French, German and Italian designers, marketing men, sociologists, economists and architects are quite as good as their US and British counterparts. Nobody, however, has yet put them into an appropriate package.

The corporate identity business then will essentially follow the path of most semi-professional consultancy businesses. It will perhaps be nearer to architecture than to advertising, nearer to management consultancy than public relations, but essentially its tone and style will be that of the consultancy activity.

Fortunately there will always be room for small, good consultancies and there will be plenty of opportunity for young, clever people with no money but quite a lot of cheek and independence to demonstrate their capabilities.

Perhaps unfortunately but equally inevitably, most design consultants in corporate identity, like most people doing most jobs everywhere, will use their modest talents to produce uninteresting and mediocre work.

Finally, I cannot see how the business can stop growing. It is after all concerned with communications, a subject in which so many of us try so hard with so little result. As organisations get bigger, which they will, and the world gets easier to travel about in, which it does, communications get more important. And in a participative society, which ours is, those who are not seen at least to be trying to communicate are damned.

Chapter 13
Getting a corporate identity—some practical advice.
How do you initiate a corporate identity programme, how do you control it, what actually happens?

If you think that your organisation may have a corporate identity problem, what can you do about it? How do you begin? Who do you go to? What does it cost? How long does it take? How do you manage it? And how do you know whether it has been a success or not? The next four chapters deal for the most part with these and other practical matters.

Companies with corporate identity problems are not often fully aware of them. They may realise that something is going wrong in two or three separate areas of the business, but they often tend to think of these things as unrelated, even when the real relationship between the problems is both close and immediate.

Sometimes what is called in psychiatric jargon 'the presenting problem' is not the real problem but only one of its manifestations, so the first piece of practical advice is that the company with corporate identity difficulties should avoid self-medication. Corporate identity is best left to experts to handle. It is not often resolved quickly, it isn't an off-the-peg operation. You can't go into a design consultants' office, pick up a corporate identity, see if it fits and then take it away.

How do you initiate a corporate identity programme? How do you control it? What actually happens?

First you get someone to help you resolve your problems. You should not appoint management consultants, or an advertising agency, or a public relations firm, or an architect, although they may help you in your selection. You should select a design consultancy company.

You may not know any design consultancies. If you don't, ask your advertising agency or PR advisers to give you some names. In Britain the Design Council has an index of consultants of various kinds including some who specialise in corporate identity. In other European countries and in the United States you will simply have to ask around. It's never a bad idea to contact a company whose corporate identity you admire and ask them how they got their job done.

You should visit two or three companies of different kinds and look at their work, which they will call their presentation, listen to what they say, see how they tackle problems, try to get some impression of the people they introduce you to, get a feeling for their size, background, experience, and on this basis try to gauge their competence and the extent to which they are suitable for you.

You will perhaps be surprised at the wide variation in fees. Small, young, hungry companies tend to charge less, but broadly speaking you get what you pay for. All design consultants' charges are based on time and this relates to their salary bills. More time on your problem spent by higher paid people costs you more money, it's really as simple as that. The big, experienced design consultancies will charge about the same as consultants in other fields, so some companies charge McKinsey prices, and others will do you a symbol for a few pounds. In the end 'you pays your money and you takes your choice'.

Consultants carry out corporate identity programmes in a series of stages. Sometimes the stages are broken down into divisions and sub-divisions, and there may appear to be four, five or even ten stages. Sometimes the job is rather more simply divided into only three. In the end though it all boils down to the same process.

The first stage is to get to know the problem and prepare a design brief. The design brief forms the basis upon which Stage 2 begins and this consists of the creation, presentation and acceptance of the design idea. When this work is approved the third stage begins; this is the development and implementation of the designs in detail so that the identity can be effectively used.

Stages 1 and 2 are interesting, even exciting. It's always fascinating to have the opportunity to go shopping for new clothes. But when Stage 2 is over and Stage 3 begins the glamour disappears and the hard slog takes its place.

The speed at which the programme is implemented depends on how dramatic the changes are, how impatient the organisation is, and how much it is prepared to pay. Cases have been known, in the petrol retailing business for example, when companies have changed their entire visible manifestations more or less overnight, well anyway over a weekend.

For the most part the implementation takes place gradually, on a replacement basis. Normally it takes about three years for a medium-sized company to emerge clearly, and rather longer for a larger organisation to start looking noticeably different.

Inevitably anyone thinking of starting a corporate identity programme wants to know what he is letting himself in for financially. The answer is curiously difficult to produce: there are two sets of costs.

First there are the consultants' costs. These will vary, as I have indicated, from job to job, from time to time, and from country to country.

Then there are the costs of doing the job. Some design consultants claim with reasonable justification that it is possible for a corporate identity programme to be self-liquidating so far as costs are concerned. The argument runs quite simply. Most organisations waste money because they buy print, packaging, stationery and signs and paint their vehicles and buildings in a haphazard, fragmented way. They do not take advantage of group purchasing power, so they get uneven results for unnecessarily high costs.

A well administered corporate identity programme produces better results for the same money or even less. From my own experience I know of a number of cases where this is true.

On the other hand, if the corporate identity programme is not used just to standardise and homogenise, if it is also used to raise standards, if it is to provide the opportunity, let's say, to provide better eating facilities or lighting levels, then the cost question has to be reviewed in a totally different light. This is one reason why it is mechanistic, and even a bit misleading, to emphasise the cost saving aspects of a corporate identity programme.

There is another factor to consider here too and this is impact. A corporate identity programme affords one of those very rare opportunities for a company to re-launch itself to everybody with whom it deals, including its own staff. To do this properly—and it's something that should be seriously thought through—will cost money, extra money that will not come from savings made in the corporate identity implementation.

Budgeting for a corporate identity programme is, like so much else to do with the subject, more complicated than it seems at first sight. In fact, the whole process of managing the development of a corporate identity programme is complex. It often goes quite badly wrong because too few people understand what a corporate identity programme is about beforehand and also because too few departments are involved. It may be worthwhile tracing the development of a hypothetical corporate identity programme to see where the trouble spots lie.

All banks have corporate identity problems. They worry about how they can attract more of the right kind of customers, about how they can improve their service so that it is better and seen to be better than that of other banks, and about how they can make their branches more effective so that they can be used to carry out a wider series of financial transactions.

Within the past few years a large number of banks have introduced corporate identity programmes to try to help them with some or all of these things. Let us examine some of the practical problems that corporate identity brings with it by picking a hypothetical bank that wants a new identity and following the design programme through its development.

Our mythical bank is known as the Bank WB. Its full name is Bank of Wales and Brittany. It was started 120 years ago by a group of financiers in Britain and France who claimed Celtic origin. In fact, the bank has no special connection with either Wales or Brittany and for the last 85 years has only used its initials. Very few people are aware of its full name.

The Bank WB is the smallest of the big British banks and its market share is static. Over the last few years it has computerised, so it is no longer so labour intensive. It has taken up marketing ideas with enthusiasm, but with no more success than any of its competitors. As the smallest of the major banks it feels vulnerable; it is looking for and failing to find a competitive edge.

It all starts when the Assistant General Manager Marketing visits an exhibition of corporate identity programmes held at The Design Centre. He is impressed and persuades his colleagues that something should be done. After some canvassing and a few presentations, the well known design consultants Thinwall & Fineline are duly appointed.

The design consultants carry out an investigation of Bank WB that is lengthy, intensive and detailed. Gavin Thinwall, a senior partner in Thinwall & Fineline, is in charge of the project. Although he is a graphic designer by training, he is also an experienced business consultant. He has a team of people working with him and together they look at the forms and stationery produced by the bank, they visit some of its 752 branches, they study marketing documents. They also have meetings with employees all the way through the bank—general managers, assistant general managers, branch managers and counter staff. They go off and talk to private and business customers, to competitors, and to people in banking throughout Europe. They end up exhausted, but with a recommendation that has the agreement of the marketing, PR and communication people: that the bank should present itself in a more modern, sympathetic way, offering a wider range of facilities to customers based on the idea of 'your money supermarket'.

This means that branches must look more friendly—more like shops, less like traditional banks. This will of course affect their interior layout and their window displays as well as their fascias and signs. It will affect advertising and literature, staff behaviour and training.

Gavin Thinwall's conclusions and his design brief are shown to the Assistant General Manager Marketing and accepted. With their design brief approved Thinwall and his team throw themselves into a frenzy of activity.

Thinwall's recommendation about advertising, literature and staff training go in one of the client's ears and out of the other. Thinwall's prime concern is to take the bank's existing graphic elements and modify them sufficiently so that they look more modern, more friendly, and more appropriate to today's circumstances. He cannot make a clean break with the past, because it is inevitable that the bank will not only want to emphasise its new personality, but also its strength, solidity, traditions and by implication its financial probity.

Thinwall has been told that, although the bank wants to look different and modern, it doesn't want to change everything and startle or shock its existing customers. In fact, part of the brief is that so far as is possible everything should stay the same. Thinwall concerns himself, despite his earlier preoccupations with the broader issues, with the graphic elements: he looks for a more friendly shade of the colour the bank has used for the best part of a hundred years. He also tries to modify the Victorian robustness of the existing symbol, which is a vulture stealing grain from a beggar, so that it remains suitably dignified and therefore likely to pass the scrutiny of the bank's board, and yet at the same time falls more into harmony with the demands of the High Street.

Within the design consultancy, Thinwall's colleagues are engaged with sign manufacturers, printers, and suppliers of other kinds in an attempt to improve the impact of the thousands of objects the bank produces, while at the same time reducing the costs of each unit wherever possible.

While Thinwall goes busily about his work, the bank's other activities go quietly trundling on. The premises department continues to commission architects to build, rebuild and refurbish its buildings. The personnel people continue to fret over the fact that the bank's image is staid and dreary and that it isn't easy to get the high flyers it wants. In the branches, managers continue to be concerned about the fact that, while the bank talks about improving its services, they know because they are at the sharp end that the actual level of service has deteriorated, is deteriorating and will, so far as they can tell, continue to do so. Apart from a fleeting and peripheral contact at the beginning of the study, and of course the interviews months before, there has been no real contact between Thinwall and these departments. None of the people in personnel or the branches or running estates has much idea what the corporate identity is about, let alone thinks it has much to do with them.

Meanwhile Thinwall goes on beavering away, and in due course he presents his scheme. The presentation is a much loved and, even in such a relatively new trade as design consultancy, a hallowed ritual. Thinwall shows his work to a few intimates in the bank who give him political guidance.

Thinwall's office prepares a thorough, careful and impressive presentation almost entirely concerned with graphics and he argues it well. The final presentation is made to an influential group that includes general managers and directors, many of whom have been well lobbied beforehand, and the scheme is accepted. Thinwall is told to get on with it.

This is where things start going wrong. Thinwall and his accomplice, the Assistant General Manager Marketing, have ignored the premises and personnel departments and concentrated on resolving some hypothetical marketing problems in graphic form. In the presentation they have shown colour slides indicating how the proposed scheme would work on the outside and inside of buildings, on cheques, stationery and other printed material, on signs, on giveaways, and on a whole series of associated items. But the place where the bank makes its real impact is not on paper but in its buildings. What matters is what it feels like to walk into a branch and deal with the staff. If, however, as we have seen, the buildings people have not been drawn into the operation, if the real point of the programme has not been explained to them, if their problems have been ignored, then they in turn will not hesitate to minimise the significance of the new visual identity programme to the people with whom they deal. To all of the architects, contractors, interior designers, signmakers and builders the premises people will explain that there has been some modest change in the bank's symbol. The potential value of the programme will have been ignored.

So what Bank WB ends up with is a minor modification to the fascias of branches—in some branches an improvement, in others no doubt not—together with some revised designs for stationery and other bits of paper. No real changes will have been made in those parts of the bank's activities that really needed it. The bank is fed up and so, for that matter, is Gavin Thinwall.

Now why is it that this sort of thing constantly happens? Why is it that, with the best will in the world, the client and his design consultant start off by trying to change the world and end up with a new symbol and a slight change in colour?

The principal reason is that most businesses are divided vertically into a number of different departments or activities and this also has the effect of isolating thinking into watertight compartments. This trend, which is naturally strong, is exacerbated by the system of financial controls that almost all organisations employ.

In order to make this point clear we can look once again at Bank WB and at the design programme worked out by Thinwall & Fineline. Let us assume that the marketing people feel that what customers want most is better service and that research confirms this.

Service is of course a broad concept—it has many implications, and it can mean many different things to different people at different times—but let's assume that the brief to Thinwall & Fineline is that the bank should become more service orientated. Gavin Thinwall and his colleagues go off and do their study bearing this in mind: they talk to bank employees, they look at branches, large and small, in towns of various sizes; they read research till it comes out of their ears; they talk to the personnel department and to the premises department. As they move around the bank they begin to see that the facilities the bank offers its own staff vary considerably: that in some branches the bank is a pleasant, agreeable place to work in, while in others it is disagreeable, hot, crowded and stuffy.

They also notice that, although the premises department is theoretically meant to offer decent conditions to staff, no norms are laid down and it is left to local architects for the most part to do what they think proper. This means that facilities, so far from gradually becoming standard, vary greatly between branches.

As Gavin Thinwall and his colleagues continue to move around they find that the personnel people feel that until the bank has something special to offer, in terms either of pay or of conditions of service, it cannot expect to recruit better people than its competitors. Clearly, if the bank isn't getting better people it is unlikely, unless its training programmes are quite remarkable and expensive, to get them to perform better than people in other banks.

So, coming back to the brief, Gavin Thinwall has to consider ways in which he can help the bank improve its service to the customer. If he has done his investigation work thoroughly he may have come to the conclusion that what he should try to do is help the personnel department to recruit better people. He could perhaps help them to do this by suggesting that consistent standards should be laid down for the physical amenities in each branch.

Thinwall might suggest that local architects should not be left to lay down any standards that they think fit, but that on the contrary the premises department should work out minimum acceptable requirements for all staff in terms of space, light, toilet facilities, recreational rooms and so on, and that these should be incorporated into the brief given to all architects working for the bank.

From a marketing point of view Thinwall could point out that the bank would be putting its money where its mouth is in its attempts to offer better service. By spending money on better amenities and publicising them, it could expect eventually to have a considerable advantage over its competitors and get better people to join its staff. When better people joined the bank, it would in the long run be able to give its customers a better service.

Now this chain of events implies that Gavin Thinwall sees his client as a whole; that he is working not just for the marketing department but for the whole organisation. But Thinwall was appointed through the influence of the bank's marketing people who were unaware of the ramifications of the problem when they appointed design consultants to carry out a corporate identity. They didn't think about premises and personnel, they didn't think to involve them, and they may not even have wanted to.

The hapless Thinwall was also a prisoner of circumstances. He was probably never fully aware of the ramifications of the problem. He was ill equipped to deal with situations outside the field of his immediate competence. When he realised what he might be letting himself in for, he had doubts about whether the bank had the imagination and the physical mechanism to evaluate a recommendation that cut across the activities of three departments— marketing, premises and personnel. These departments in most companies, not just banks, tend to think of themselves as separate organisations with little common ground: they have different suppliers, different traditions, different ways of doing things, and their own jealously guarded financial budgets, which represent their base of power. So Thinwall confined his recommendations to the field his client anticipated and with which he was familiar, and not too many awkward questions were asked.

The point I am making here is really quite simple but very important: unless personnel and premises, and appropriate people from other departments too, are brought into discussions about corporate identity at a very early stage, they are almost certain to regard them as frivolous and trivial exercises typical of a marketing department that is swayed by every breeze of fashion. Equally the marketing people, conditioned to think of corporate identity almost entirely in terms of graphics, are likely to regard as irrelevant proposals that do not have a clear and immediate impact on marketing.

If corporate identity extends over so many activities and involves so many departments, how can it be managed? The problem of interface is very difficult and complicated and is one of many that have not yet been solved. All of us involved in corporate identity programmes are groping for solutions. How is it possible to compare what is spent on refurbishing buildings with what is spent on advertising? It may not be like comparing apples with pears—the two things are not necessarily as distant from each other as all that—but in most companies there is a violent resistance to such comparisons, because they appear to strike at the power base of a department.

What went wrong with our friend Thinwall and the Bank WB was that the job was managed at the wrong level. The management of corporate identity should operate at two levels. At one level, corporate identity is part of corporate strategy. If the corporate identity programme is going to be effectively integrated into long-term planning, if it is going to be a major influence on the culture of the organisation, if it is going to affect decisions over a broad spectrum of activities, then inevitably it has to be managed from the top—the chief executive will have to bear the ultimate responsibility for it.

The amount of his time it takes will of course vary according to the nature of the organisation, its size, the complexity of the problem, and the stage of development the programme has reached.

At the second level, control is more difficult to resolve. Corporate identity is seen as having something to do with advertising, public relations or marketing, and it is therefore often instigated and managed by PR, marketing or advertising departments. While for the most part people with these disciplines and backgrounds tend to be sympathetic to some aspects of corporate identity activity, it is also true that marketing and, more particularly, advertising people frequently interpret corporate identity in a rather narrow sense. They can sometimes inhibit the development of a corporate identity programme, particularly over activities in a company other than those with which they are familiar.

So what other possibilities of control are there? At the moment people are discussing with great enthusiasm the new profession of design manager. The excitement being generated by this concept is not dissimilar to that which heralded the arrival of that all singing, all dancing genius the marketing man a generation ago. This polymath will look after all aspects of a company's design output, from its buildings to its products, to its printed matter. He will liaise with personnel, product, marketing, building, sales and financial people. He will be involved in corporate strategy at one level and brand management at another.

The design manager concept may be sensible in principle, although I am by no means sold on the idea. It has, however, one major drawback: there are very few design managers around. Where do you recruit them from? How do you train them? What sort of age, experience and background should they have? What budgets should they control? All these questions are being hotly debated, but for practical purposes, for the next 10 years or so, there won't be enough design managers around for everyone to notice, and those few who do exist will be tentatively, tactfully and furtively pushing forward the limits of their individual power.

Are there any other possibilities then? Well, there is the committee system. We all know what disadvantages this has: it is cumbersome, it takes decisions very slowly, and when they emerge they're often wrong. Above all, it is a breeding ground for internal politics. But the committee system also has one considerable advantage: it consists of at least two people. This means or should mean that more than one department or activity or function will be represented on it, which in turn means that the identity programme need not be the sole preserve of one corporate department. It means that information about the nature of a corporate identity has at least a fair chance of being disseminated throughout the organisation, and therefore that the programme will not be totally lopsided.

Perhaps the least unsatisfactory way of handling an identity programme is to make it the responsibility of someone who really cares about it and understands its implications. It does not particularly matter what his discipline and previous training has been; in a sense, if it is legal or financial or engineering or planning, so much the better—he will not have, or be seen to have, prejudices that influence his judgement. He will above all be committed to the programme, and see it as an opportunity both for the company and himself.

He should be a senior, experienced man, he will need assistants, and he will need to know his way around the company, to know who seems to matter and who really matters. He will need to be near the centre of power, and he will need to be persuasive, imaginative and tenacious. His precise title, rank and position, and whether or not he controls a budget or merely influences those who control it, will depend upon the nature of the organisation, but he is going to be involved in a job that, although it will vary according to the stages through which the operation passes, will take up the greater part of his time for some years.

The corporate identity programme should then be the responsibility of the chief executive at the top level and of a committee or senior manager at the organisational level. In this way the misfortunes suffered by Gavin Thinwall with the Bank WB can be mitigated, if not totally avoided.

Chapter 14
Stage 1 — investigation
Who are we and what are we like?

The first stage of a corporate identity programme involves an examination of the presence of the company. The idea is to start from what exists. What is the organisation like now? What does it look like? What do people think about it? How much do they know about it? What are its products like? How does it compare or how is it thought to compare with competitors? What are its strengths and its weaknesses? When all that is clear, it is important to determine what the ambitions of the organisation are. Where does it think it is going? How does it think it is getting there?

The next step is to determine the way in which the proposed corporate identity programme can help the organisation achieve its ambitions.

The major part of the first stage is finding out about the company. For the most part this means talking to people and listening to them.

The investigation stage of a corporate identity programme is about quality rather than quantity; it is not about head counting. It is much more like investigative journalism than conventional market research.

It usually takes a sensitive and intelligent observer to pick up all the dimensions of an interview.

It is sometimes difficult to isolate one part of the investigation process from another. My colleague Michael Wolff once interviewed the personnel manager of an advanced engineering company. The rain dripped from a hole in the roof of the unheated, prefabricated structure where they sat together. It slowly trickled onto the head of the personnel manager and ran down his nose. Apparently oblivious of this, he explained to Michael Wolff, who was huddled in the folds of his sheepskin coat struggling to keep warm and dry, that what they wanted in the company were young people really in sympathy with what Harold Wilson had just called 'the white-hot technological revolution'.

The sentiments exchanged in the interview were, as Wolff pointed out, unexceptionable in themselves. But the combination of the interview, the opinions and the ambitions expressed, contrasted with the pitifully inadequate surroundings, revealed much more of the story.

Having lunch in a canteen and talking to a German workers' council where three or four people speak at the same time has a significance well beyond what is actually said. The significance relates to where the interview is held, how people talk, how much they talk, how discreet or indiscreet they are, and what attitudes are both to one another and to the management.

Who then should be responsible for the investigation stage? Should a market research company do it, or should the design consultants look after it? There are some research companies that can help with this kind of work; others are too mechanistic, too obsessed with head counting and percentages to be of much use. Some research organisations that are qualitative rather than quantitative in their approach are sometimes unable to produce a sufficient number of really highly skilled interviewers to do the job properly.

Design consultancy companies can also be inadequate at the investigation stage. The designer's obsession with what it looks like and changing it whatever it is sometimes seems to overwhelm his sense of proportion. On the other hand design consultants who employ people experienced in investigative techniques—journalists, marketing people, even anthropologists, people who can talk and look and listen, even do all three, who can transmit not just what was said but the atmosphere in which it took place—these are the people who are invaluable in making the investigation stage effective.

Then again there is no substitute for personal involvement. Two hundred pages of second-hand reported information are rarely worth one hour of first-hand conversation. The design consultant must have some personal involvement with the client company at a variety of levels, otherwise he won't really have a feeling for it.

The need for personal involvement must come first, which is why it is preferable for design consultants to organise and so far as possible carry out the investigation operation, although there is always room to work in conjunction with research companies. An experienced design consultancy will have carried out enough investigations to know how to plan and execute them. The design consultant may need to call upon outside help, he may have a panel of researchers upon which to draw, but he should run the investigation, carry out many of the interviews and the other monitoring activities and prepare the report for the client.

Working out who should be interviewed is important. The people who are to be interviewed should be representative of all the groups with which the organisation has some kind of relationship. Audiences for a corporate identity programme are divided into two groups: internal, that is the people inside the organisation; and external, that is the people outside it.

So far as internal audiences are concerned, it is often convenient to follow the diagonal slice selection method. This simply means cutting a diagonal slice down the company's structure and interviewing people on it. These interviews will probably have to be supplemented at various levels: it is of course vital to interview the chief executive and to talk to people at or near the top in most departments.

If the organisation has workers' councils it may be worth while talking to them; it's certainly important to look at things from the shop floor as well as the executive floor. It's also vital not to concentrate too heavily on the head office and on the centre. Here again the temptation is to stay near the power source and be influenced by it. In fact, if a company has several factories or sales points or depots, it's important to visit enough of these to get a feeling for their emotional and physical atmosphere.

Where an international company is being studied it is essential to visit a number of world-wide activities. The reputation the company and its products enjoy in one country is frequently different in others and sometimes these variations can be very dramatic.

People at the centre don't always know the truth about the company's problems and opportunities in the various countries in which it operates. Sometimes the company operates under different names in different countries, sometimes it has varying market shares. Often the cultural climate varies and even standards of quality and methods of marketing may be different.

It is usually assumed that once the design consultants come in the homogenisation process has begun. Quite often, though, there are good arguments for local companies keeping their own names, local operations staying different, and for local culture remaining independent.

The growth of nationalism and the antagonism to the multinational idea are very important phenomena and cannot simply be brushed aside in the interests of neatness and homogeneity. Furthermore, many international organisations have a minority, or even a majority local shareholding whose feelings have to be considered.

In considering what to recommend for international activities with differing names and visual styles, the consultant, and for that matter the holding company too, usually only takes one factor into consideration: whether homogenisation will affect market penetration. If the answer is that a change of name or branding won't in the long run damage the market position, the recommendation to go ahead is usually made.

But there are three other factors that are equally important but which are rarely given sufficient consideration. The first of these concerns the internal morale of the local organisation. How independent does it feel? How strong are the currents of nationalism in the country? How strong is the dislike of multinationals? Would trade unions exploit the change to the disadvantage of the company? Who do people in the local company feel they are working for? What would happen if the atmosphere changed? What would local shareholders feel? What might the government of the host country feel?

The second factor is even more difficult to quantify, but it is just as important as the other two. What benefits does the local operation derive from its association with the parent company? Does it get technological help, advanced equipment, does it get financial assistance, does it get help in training its people to much higher standards than the local competition? Put another way, why should the local company immolate itself as an entity, what will it get in exchange? Will the benefits be illusory or real?

The third factor concerns how the centre can actually direct the activities of the operating units. To what extent does it have the nervous system to do so?

So far as the mechanics are concerned, the whole study should begin with a note from the chief executive. This should be sent to all managers telling them that consultants have been appointed to work on a corporate identity programme and explaining what that is and what it involves. The note should say that the consultants will be talking to people in the company at various levels and that the discussions will be kept confidential. Naturally people being interviewed are expected to express their opinions freely and openly.

Once the note has been issued, the individuals selected and the discussions started, there is rarely any problem about getting people to talk. Everybody likes to talk about his work, his attitudes towards his company, how it is run, what's wrong with it, what's right with it, how it compares with other companies he has been in, the different factions, the lack of direction, the waste of resources, the dependence on one man, the strength of marketing, the weakness of production, the emotional impact of the merger and the extent to which there is a really new spirit.

Each interview should be conducted in such a way so that the consultant gently leads the discussion from one subject to another. It is usually best to start by asking people to describe their job and explain briefly how they got it. This introduction is always helpful; on the factual side it says whether the man has been with the company a long time, and if the company has merged, with which of the partners he has spent most of his career. It also indicates whether he talks a lot, whether he is overtly out to impress. ('After 12 years as managing director in Pakistan, where we had some modest successes, I was made Eastern Region Manager based at Bury St Edmunds.') It indicates fairly quickly whose side he is on, apart from his own.

From this point the discussion can take a whole range of directions. Has the organisation changed over the last few years, for the better or worse? Has the market share fallen or improved? Were the mergers, takeovers or whatever necessary? How were they carried out? What have the effects been? Which side dominates the new organisation? Will there be further mergers? Is the new management handling things in the right way? What would he do if he was in charge? How has morale been affected? Should there have been more factory closures? What are the strengths and weaknesses of the company? How does it compare with the competition? Is it very political? Are communications satisfactory? What is product quality like? How do marketing and production get on? How is the business moving? What products will it be making in, say, five years or ten years? It is often helpful to trace the development of an important recent decision.

The list of questions, all of which are leading, all of which enable the discussions to be directed into fields that are of particular interest to the investigation, and some of which cover the same ground, must be carefully worked out.

When it comes to interviewing outsiders a rather different situation prevails. However closely involved with an organisation an outsider may be, he has a more detached attitude towards it than do its employees. Furthermore, because all of us when we are interviewed have a tendency to want to please, we may be inclined to affect an interest in and a knowledge of the subject which is greater than we really have. For these reasons interviews with people outside the company are usually different in intensity, if not in kind, from those with insiders.

What sort of outsiders should be interviewed? How many of each sort? Within each category, how should individuals be picked and interviews arranged? This must be determined by the individual study. Usually it's desirable to talk to some customers—in the case of consumer companies trade customers, in the case of industrial companies direct customers. It's also important to see suppliers. They are involved in a network of intrigue, gossip and rumour. They can spot if the company seems to be in trouble because their bills aren't paid so quickly. They can compare the efficiency of purchasing systems and quality control as well as the quantities of raw materials purchased by all their customers.

Competitors are also worth seeing. At an operating level they too tend to live in a world of rumour and half truth, although at more elevated levels the atmosphere between competitors becomes much friendlier—to the extent that in some industries the competition seems to disappear in reality if not in appearance at the top!

It is usually worthwhile talking to financial journalists. Like the rest of us, they react in a partial and prejudiced way according to the experiences that they have had—it's extraordinary how often an unhappy experience with an electric iron or a bad interview with a PR man leads to a blanket condemnation of a massive industrial enterprise. On the other hand, financial journalists should have some kind of perspective of an industry as a whole.

Very often a company wants to know what people in the financial world think of it. Here the problems of selection are particularly acute. Many professional managers for the institutions are extremely well informed.

On the other hand, the well known gulf between industry and finance is often clearly exemplified. It is astonishing how little leaders of the financial world seem to know about the size and activities of companies in which they have a financial interest.

There are usually some other categories of outside organisations to consider. The whole complex of employer/employee relations through university appointments boards, trade unions, local labour exchanges and job shops is one group. Community relations, through local newspapers, local and regional authorities, local community groups, is another. The research and development activity, through independent research organisations, trade associations, university research institutes, is a third. Advertising agencies, accountants, research organisations and marketing consultants can sometimes be very important sources of knowledge. How does one approach these various groups? How does one pick the individuals and what questions does one ask them?

In the first place, somebody has to sit down and work out which groups of people are worth seeing; the steering committee or manager for the project should do this. Then the individuals in each category have to be selected. Some of these emerge by virtue of their job or their position in the industry, others are more difficult to pick.

Interviews with outsiders can either be arranged openly, in which case the reaction and response of the interviewee will inevitably be biased, or they can be arranged in some other way, in which case replies and responses are less likely to be prejudiced and are sometimes more valuable. Confidentiality must of course be respected.

A little elementary subterfuge may sometimes be necessary. If I claim that I want to talk to, say, a stockbroker acquaintance about the machine tool industry because I have a client who is thinking of making an acquisition in the business when in fact I am interested in the stockbroker's opinion about the specific company by whom I am retained, this fairly simple and harmless ruse will be sufficient to give me cover, and it will ensure that the hypothetical stockbroker will air his opinion without prejudice. In general, meetings of this kind should be informal and the atmosphere created should be like a chat, apparently covering as wide a range of topics as possible.

Interviewing is a tough and exhausting business. It's useful to have a team of three or four people working on a large project. This team should brief themselves effectively and meet regularly to review their progress and check one another's impressions. In a large, complex project it is not unusual to interview 100 internal people and the same number of outsiders over, say, a three-month period.

While the interviews are taking place, the visual appearance of the company and its products must be examined. Its buildings and signs should be looked at. Working conditions in different units should be examined and where appropriate photographed. The company's packaging and products should be collected, collated and photographed, its letterheads and other stationery in all group companies should be gathered together and compared with those of the competition. Advertising and other promotional material should also be collected, examined and compared with that produced by the industry as a whole.

Members of the team should attempt to simulate what happens when someone joins the company. How is he interviewed, what pieces of paper does he get, what sort of induction process takes place? Other members of the team may well investigate buying or selling or service procedures. The idea behind this is to understand how the company behaves in different situations, and whether its behaviour is clear and consistent.

In addition to this, purchasing systems should be examined. Who controls the budgets? Why are apparently arbitrarily high or low figures spent on items of equipment? Who decides, say, the repainting budget, the printing budget, the advertising budget? Who monitors the quality of materials of all kinds purchased? Are there common purchasing standards throughout the organisation?

During the course of this phase of the work there must be regular meetings between the consultancy and the client to monitor progress. In particular, the long-term aims of the corporate identity programme must be regularly reviewed. For the most part the work carried out in Stage 1 is aimed at examining the existing situation, to provide a clear understanding of the base from which the attempt to change is being made.

So far, what has been established is, first, how the organisation is currently perceived by everybody who comes into contact with it, and second, why it is perceived in the way that it is. This is likely to be useful and salutary information; it will probably help the organisation not only with its identity, but also with very many other aspects of its activities.

Before Stage 1 ends, however, another step has to be taken. The organisation under scrutiny has ambitions, targets, intentions; it has some sense of direction. The chances are that a corporate identity programme will not be the only activity being undertaken to move the company forward.

Almost every company has a plan that it attempts to pursue, even if this has not been formalised. Some companies have a lot of plans that are mutually contradictory and they try to pursue them all.

The plan, whatever it is and however tight or loose its shape, gives an indication of what the company wants to become. Corporate intentions, however vaguely or precisely formulated, should be thoroughly discussed. When this has been done all the elements of the first stage of the corporate identity programme are present.

First of all, the investigation will have indicated how the organisation sees itself at various levels. Second, it will have indicated how it is seen by others; any disparities between what it thinks of itself and what others think of it will become apparent. Third, the investigation will have shown how the organisation presents itself visually and, if disparities exist between how it is actually seen and how it wants to be seen, why these disparities exist. The discussions with those responsible for the future of the company will have rounded off the situation; they will reveal what the company wants to be and what its ambitions are.

All that now remains to be done in the first stage is to work out how the corporate identity programme can help the organisation achieve its ambitions. It will do this by making it feel and look different. It may involve a change of name or names, it may involve an entirely new identity, or it may involve a modification of an existing one. It may involve the creation of a new branding structure. In one way or another it will probably involve some or all of the techniques that have been discussed earlier.

The convention of the trade is that the first two stages of work end with a presentation. Stage 1 therefore might conceivably end with a formal presentation to the board of the company, showing the existing situation, discussing the future ambitions of the company, and explaining how the corporate identity programme can help to achieve them.

Presentations of this kind, about which I shall have a word or two to say later on, are perhaps more valuable when there is something more constructive to show, and it may be advisable to defer a major presentation to the end of the second stage of the programme, when there is much more to see. In any event, whether there is a presentation or not, the first stage must end with agreement on the way in which the corporate identity programme can help the organisation achieve its objectives, and with the development of a design brief. The design brief forms the basis for the creative work that is carried out in Stage 2.

Because the design brief is a vital document in the development of the corporate identity programme a lot of care is lavished on it. It is often written, rewritten and then given another polish or two. Sometimes, however, the brief can be a simple four or five line note, and occasionally it isn't even written down at all—it's something that everyone has talked about so much that putting it down on paper seems superfluous.

The design brief outlines what the identity programme is expected to do. Is it intended to build a strong internal identity or external identity or both? What kind of identity is it aiming to build up? Without getting too involved in clichés like dynamic, powerful, aggressive and friendly, what kind of a personality is it intending to emphasise? To what extent is it designed to affect the marketing apparatus? Will it interfere with brand identification, will it supersede all existing brand identification, or will there be a sliding scale of involvement, varying from none at all to remote, to medium, to close, to overwhelming?

Where will the identity be applied? Across the whole company, only to part of it, to graphics, to products, to buildings? Is the company going totally and rapidly to change its imagery or will the change be gradual and hardly perceptible? Will there be a completely new corporate name, will there be brand name changes, will there be rationalisation?

What other changes will take place in the company at the same time—a further merger that the new identity must embrace, a redirection or a reduction of activities?

The design brief can be long and detailed or short and sharp. In either case, it forms the basis for the next step, which is getting the design idea.

Chapter 15
Stage 2—design
Pressures under which designers work.
Getting the right scheme.

The differences between some abstract symbols are so small as to be barely visible, so it was inevitable that one of them should eventually crash headlong into another. It was also likely by the law of averages that it should happen in America, where symbols are used so profusely. What was not so certain was that the affair would be so rich in irony. It happened in the radio and television network industry, between a David in Nebraska and a Goliath in New York. The Goliath design consultancy involved was the daddy of them all, Lippincott & Margulies.

L & M was commissioned to produce a corporate identity programme for the National Broadcasting Company, a subsidiary of the RCA company for whom it had earlier produced corporate identity work. After much effort and a lot of money L & M created as part of its programme exactly the same symbol as one designed for a tiny radio and TV network in Nebraska, which had spent practically no time or money on the job. Inevitably both Lippincott & Margulies and NBC emerged from the incident with egg on their faces. The massive efforts made in New York and London by the L & M offices, involving psychiatrists, market researchers and above all graphic designers, two of whom in L & M's offices on either side of the Atlantic produced the identical symbol, looked absurd next to the work done for the little Nebraska educational network whose symbol was produced by one staff man.

NBC   NEBRASKA

New York magazine in its issue of January 26, 1976 was particularly scathing, not just about Walter Margulies,

Lippincott & Margulies and NBC, but about the corporate identity business as a whole. It quoted Tom Wolfe's observations on the subject when, some years before, he had been one of the judges in a design competition sponsored by the American Institute of Graphic Arts. He wrote about his experiences in the July 17, 1972 issue of *New York*. These are some of the things he said which, on the occasion of the NBC debacle, four years later, *New York* published again:

'... These abstract logos, which a company ... is supposed to put on everything from memo pads to the side of its 50-storey building, make absolutely no impact—conscious or unconscious—upon its customers or the general public, except insofar as they create a feeling of vagueness of confusion. I'm talking about the prevailing mode of *abstract* logos. Pictorial logos or written logos are a different story. Random House (the little house), Alfred Knopf (the borzoi dog), the old Socony-Vacuum flying red horse, or the written logos of Coca-Cola or Hertz—they stick in the mind and create the desired effect of instant recognition ("identity"). Abstract logos are a dead loss in that respect, and yet millions continue to be poured into the design of them. Why? Because the conversion to a total-design abstract logo formation somehow makes it possible for the head of the corporation to tell himself: "I'm modern, up to date, with it, a man of the future. I've *streamlined* this old baby." '

L & M and NBC were unlucky in that their clash was more public and humiliating than most, but a glance at any book on symbols will show that this situation is not at all uncommon.

What is it all about then? Why are graphic designers still busily scribbling away at stylised flasks symbolising the powerful modern chemical company busying itself with Man's Future but human enough to remember its Humble Origins? Why are they still producing stylised sheaves of some unspecified grain for food companies, indicating that the organisation has an involvement of however remote a kind with agriculture and Dear Old Dame Nature Herself by whose Bounty we all live? Above all, why are they still churning out these symbols consisting of initial letters tormented into a bizarre shape and ending with an arrow, preferably pointing upwards and slightly to the right, indicative of Progress, Dynamism and a controlled but powerful thrust towards what is clearly a Better and Brighter Future?

Why is it that the design idea that ultimately emerges is so often banal and trite? Is this naive rubbish the best that we can do?

Is it ever possible to achieve anything different and better? Is it desirable? Does it do the organisation any good to have an advanced visual identity? Or is corporate identity really, despite all the talk, just a simple labelling device saying 'Here I am, look at me'?

In order to understand why so much of the work produced is so banal it's worth examining the pressures that influence designers. These derive from two sources: from the designers themselves and from their clients. The pressures to which designers subject themselves come from their desire to express themselves creatively, to produce something they themselves think well of, that will satisfy their clients and impress their peer group—other designers.

The pressures from the client are different. Consider the state of mind of executives in a big business dealing with corporate identity. Unless they are exceptionally self-confident or have been involved in a corporate identity programme before, they will on the one hand be very enthusiastic to produce something new, exciting and different, but on the other need to cling to the familiar, to what they know has worked well for somebody else.

Most people coming for the first time to an activity where decisions on colour, shape and style are called for are reluctant to trust their own judgement. It's bad enough picking a tie, worse making a criticism of a painting, unless it has a recognised authority's seal of approval, but nightmarish to make observations on a design that will, if approved, ultimately appear on millions of objects associated with the organisation and therefore inevitably have considerable commercial repercussions.

Although the decisions that have to be taken are commercial, and although they are among the factors that will affect the future of the company, they are rarely quantifiable by normal commercial criteria. In this kind of situation most executives naturally cling to the familiar, to what has worked in the past. So while the executive says he wants something different and new, what he really wants is something that looks like what other people have, so that he doesn't run the risk of looking foolish—of putting on the Emperor's New Clothes. Inevitably, this is a pressure in the direction of conformity.

Another pressure is that most large organisations want to say the same thing: they want to be friendly, progressive, modern, efficient—human and dynamic. These worn out and meaningless verbal clichés have visual equivalents—that's where these arrows darting desperately about the place come from. The visual clichés are familiar and reassuring to an organisation embarking on a corporate identity programme in an insecure or uncertain mood.

The situation is exacerbated by the assumption underlying corporate thinking, which is that the corporation has somehow conquered nature. Corporations want to imply that they are calm, reasoned and disciplined, that their judgements and decisions are based on rational and unemotional assessments, that they are infallible. This cool arrogance reaches its apogee architecturally in terms of huge concrete and steel structures furnished as an elite fantasy world of chrome, glass, steel and Barcelona chairs.

This executive clutter underlines and exacerbates the corporation's separateness from the rest of society. It is as irrational and emotional a display as that of Louis XIV's Versailles and is carried out for the same reasons.

The intricate combination of pressures makes a massive impact on the design consultant and his work. It is a huge, brooding, omnipresent influence. It partially accounts for all those corporate identity programmes that end up saying 'Me big powerful corporation—you small stupid consumer'.

But there are also other influences on the graphic designer. Of these perhaps the most important is the designer's own training and background and his desire for recognition in his own world.

Applied design of all kinds in most countries has been influenced by the work of the Bauhaus. As is often the way of these things, some of the enthusiastic, well meaning disciples of the Bauhaus movement have so distorted its teachings that much of its original content is no longer recognisable. The Bauhaus movement has been made the scapegoat for the wholesale rejection of decoration and frivolity in favour of simplicity and sobriety. In its trivialised, oversimplified, bastardised commercial form this has too often meant that straight lines are in and squiggles are out. Perhaps the Swiss school of graphic designers and typographers has much to answer for here. Swiss typographical designers are the self-appointed guardians of some Bauhaus traditions. Not only have they been the principal perpetrators of a considerable amount of arid and clinical design, but they have also had their dreary stuff widely publicised.

Even now in some less enlightened quarters Swiss typography, with its compulsive need to neaten, tidy up and too often to render illegible, is regarded as the only worthwhile typographical tradition. The Bauhaus traditions or the corruptions of it in which most successful graphic designers have been trained, and which in unsympathetic hands are so often cold and inhuman, are particularly attractive to the big company that wants to look cool and rational. For this kind of organisation, so-called functional design is qualitatively and emotionally superior to any other sort.

The situation is compounded by three other factors. First, graphic designers rarely consider the overall framework in which their work will appear. They will almost invariably have uppermost in their minds things like letterheads, forms, vehicles, signs—objects upon which it is possible for them to make an immediate impact.

Second, they try in everyone's interest to keep the design solution as simple as possible. Most designers have come across the ingenuity that is displayed in distorting and destroying quite basic design programmes, which is why some experienced designers try to produce schemes whose implementation can be carried out on the painting by numbers principle.

Third, the scale of some jobs, the amount of detailed work involved, the series of presentations, of committees, of different management groups, sometimes causes designers to lose sight of the overall objective. The content of the work gets lost on the way.

All of these factors then—the company's need for something safe and reassuring, the corporate desire for the clean, austere and superhuman look, the distorted and degenerate Bauhaus tradition, the designer's need to impress his peer group, the attempt to keep things simple, the sheer scale of much of the work required—conspire to produce the dull, boring, repetitive, cliché-ridden designs full of superficial graphic puns and silly tricks that are the basis of so many corporate identity programmes today.

In this kind of atmosphere, selling a good, simple design idea and making it work is a daunting prospect. The number of really good, original design programmes produced in the last few years can be counted on the fingers of one hand—well, maybe both hands.

Whether the job is large or small, complex or simple, the design consultant needs to develop not just a symbol and a few colours, but a visual system that allows the organisation to express moods and make a series of interrelated statements. Normally the visual system the design consultant develops will consist of a series of visual elements which will, when put together in a variety of different ways, allow the organisation to make appropriate statements in different tones of voice.

The elements consist of one or more colours, typefaces, symbols and logotypes—in effect a special way of writing a word. At its simplest the visual elements can consist of one symbol, one colour and a line of type; at its most complex it may be made up of a whole series of base colours, say one for each division or company or brand, a series of supporting colours, a range of up to 20 or more symbols, a whole series of alphabets and a further group of logotypes.

In the interests of clarity and economy, everybody likes to keep things as simple as possible, but a corporate identity programme is designed to be a manifestation of corporate policy. If the policy is to maintain a complex hierarchy of brands and companies within an overall framework then appropriate arrangements must be made to enable this to happen.

All of this work takes some time, usually months rather than weeks, and occasionally years rather than months. While the design consultant tries out his ideas, scribbles them on paper and thinks about them, he will have a series of regular meetings with the representatives of the organisation for whom he is working to show them what he is doing. No design consultant can work successfully by himself; he needs a close relationship with his client.

The relationship between the client and the design consultant, particularly at the creative stage, is one of the key factors in arriving at an appropriate design solution. The design consultant and his client can jointly monitor what has been done to see if it is likely to work technically, discuss whether it is likely to get through politically, and talk about the practical problems involved. As the design scheme develops, a number of people from the client organisation can be involved in the programme so that they can identify themselves with it.

How, therefore, can decent creative standards be achieved? The design consultant must have imagination, self-confidence and practical experience, he must have the courage to say what he doesn't know as well as what he does. He should always remember that his job is to help the client achieve some fairly straightforward intentions, like increasing his market share, creating better internal relationships and so on. The designer is not to use present-day jargon simply on an ego trip. There has to be mutual trust and respect between him and his client. The design consultant must be able to feel that his ideas, assuming that they are practical and appropriate, will be accepted and will be effectively implemented. The client must be genuinely open to ideas, ready to argue positively and not negatively, and, if he is convinced about the idea, he must put his weight behind it.

Eventually the design idea has to be presented, usually formally. At this point is must be shown both in its component parts and as a finished scheme on a wide spectrum of objects.

Corporations, like people, like to know in detail what they are buying. Some people have difficulty in imagining what a thing will look like before it has been done. Many presentations are therefore pieces of theatre aimed at showing, by a mixture of logical argument and seductively presented pictures and text, the weaknesses of the present situation and the opportunities for the future. Some presentations use the most elaborate audio-visual techniques; others simply involve a few rough drawings.

The method that seems likely to be the most persuasive is the one to use.

All the real work, the real discussions, should have been done weeks and months before. The relationship between the client and the consultant should have been so close that by the time the presentation takes place the work shown should be an amalgam of the design consultant's thoughts and ideas and the client's practical experience.

The formal presentation is sometimes made to the board of the company well after it has been seen and approved by those in the company who are closely involved in the project, including, if things have been properly managed, the chief executive. Sometimes the presentation is not seen by the chief executive first, and then there may be problems. Politics in this, as in so many other similar situations, matter a great deal. The people who are important need to be lobbied and a public showing, cold, can invite trouble.

In a large organisation anything between one and 20 presentations may be needed. A company with a series of divisions and subsidiaries will certainly want to present its proposed new identity to all of them. Whether the managers of the subsidiaries and divisions are invited in order to discuss and either approve or reject, or simply to discuss and make observations, depends on the company, the personality of the chief executive and his colleagues, and the nature of the enterprise.

Usually a new corporate identity programme is part of a package of reform and modifications, and therefore the climate within the company is often about right to accept it. If the design consultant has sufficiently broad vision and has done his homework, he will be able to point out that what is being proposed is not simply a few superficial changes to the graphics of the company but an integral part of the fundamental corporate reorientation that is taking place. The design programme is a catalyst enabling at least some parts of the corporate strategy to be achieved. Usually therefore discussions revolve not so much around what should be done in principle—if the consultant has done his job properly there isn't a lot of disagreement about that—but about what is proposed in detail. Most people are concerned about how the proposals will affect them personally—how their status, title and prestige will be affected—so detailed proposals are always examined in a personal way.

The chances are that the design proposals will be modified in one respect or another before they get through, but ultimately a corporation that is serious about its future will recognise that the corporate identity will help it to achieve its objectives. Eventually then, the chances are that the design programme will be accepted.

Chapter 16
Stage 3—implementation
Saying it doesn't make it happen—but doing it properly does.

All of the work—the investigation, the analysis, the brief, the design idea and development—leads up to implementation—doing the job. It is the most important part of the whole elaborate corporate identity apparatus and somehow it seldom works as it should.

Why is this? Why are so few corporate identity programmes implemented properly? Why are so many of them badly and ineffectively carried out? Why is it that the design manual, the coffee-table book, is so often the most thoroughly implemented part of the whole programme? The answers are complex; they don't reside in one place or in one person.

There are five reasons why corporate identity programmes go wrong. The significance of these varies according to the size of a company, its market position and the personalities running it, but they are all important.

In the first place, when the corporate identity programme reaches the implementation stage it is old hat for top management. They have been living with it for months, maybe even for years. For them the excitement is over, they just want the job done. Except in very rare cases, top management is no longer directly involved.

So implementation goes into the corporate machine, which raises the second problem: unless the nature of the corporate identity and its long-term objectives have been explained with skill and care to those who are responsible for carrying it out, it is inevitable that they won't properly understand it and will take mechanistic decisions that may well be contrary to the spirit, if not the letter, of the corporate identity programme.

In any successful corporate identity programme the men at the top affirm and re-affirm their interest. In ones that don't work properly, they don't.

The third factor relates to morale. Where a corporation faces basic morale problems it is inevitable that the implementation process will suffer. No corporate identity programme, however well intentioned, can do that much for the American railways system, or for that matter for British Rail. The plain fact is that British Rail is still painfully shrinking, that its position in relation to any potential co-ordinated transport system is uncertain, and that inevitably therefore its morale remains poor. This is of course reflected in the manner in which the implementation of its corporate identity is carried out. Corporate identity is not, after all, the universal panacea; it will not turn bad into good overnight. If some British Rail stations are uncared for and some British Rail employees are unkempt, ill informed and apathetic, this is because morale is low, and morale is low because of uncertainty. No identity programme can fundamentally alter that.

The fourth reason for the malfunction of implementation programmes relates very much to the culture of organisations. The implementation of a corporate identity programme involves understanding its intention and translating that intention into reality. But quite often the discipline of the corporate identity does not appear to be compatible with that of the organisation. If the discipline of the identity implies 'Buy the best at key points' and the tradition of the organisation demands 'Buy the cheapest— always', unless the educational process has been lengthy and profound the identity will lose and the standard reflexes win. Only when the disciplines involved in the corporate identity programme are absorbed into the traditional culture of the company will the implementation work. This problem is especially acute at the periphery of the company, in its branches and its smaller subsidiaries, where there has been less explanation and less indoctrination and where the traditional culture is stronger.

The final reason, and perhaps the most important of all, is that a corporate identity implementation programme is genuinely very difficult to control. It cuts across traditionally separate activities, it implies a different and in some senses contradictory set of standards from that normally applied in organisations, it implies taking a wider range of factors than usual into account when making decisions, and above all its impact is difficult to quantify.

All this means that the demands made upon those responsible for running an implementation programme can be very great. Modern management systems have not allowed for this discipline within the organisation's structure. There is no corporate identity manager or design manager, to liaise, for example, with a product and brand manager to see that the products the company produces accurately reflect the style of the company; to liaise with a personnel executive about the way in which the style of the organisation emerges in recruitment literature; or to liaise with a buyer in a car factory to see that the standard of the door handles he orders accurately relates to the imagery of the car brand for which he is carrying out the purchase. All this is either left to individuals to work out painfully for themselves or, more often, ignored. The whole business of corporate identity control hardly exists.

It is for these five reasons that, for the most part, implementation is shoddy and superficial.

Implementation involves an infinity of detailed work: each item that is used by or produced for an organisation has to go through a complex chain of controls to meet marketing, functional, economic and corporate identity criteria. Each time the organisation commissions something, whether it is a new building, a new pack or a pair of cufflinks, consideration of the balance of a whole series of factors must take place. Each time one of these factors outbalances any of the others, problems arise. In one sense then, the implementation of a corporate identity programme is the sum of a vast mass of these mostly minor decisions.

Some companies have considerable internal resources to cope with these problems—design departments, publicity and promotion sections. But, however large these departments are, they can never hope to handle all the work which a company needs in its day-to-day business.

The design consultant can also make a contribution, but he is best used to establish principles, to carry out a monitoring operation, and perhaps work on a few key jobs that refresh the company's mind about what it wanted the identity for in the first place.

In addition, most large corporations have many hundreds, sometimes thousands, of suppliers whose work has a profound and lasting impact on its identity. There are printers, builders, vehicle painters, architects, interior designers, advertising agencies, sales promotion consultants, exhibition stand designers and constructors, uniform suppliers, packaging manufacturers, machinery and equipment suppliers, suppliers of raw materials and many, many others who sell to the corporation.

If the corporate identity programme is to work effectively, somehow or other all of these people, both the people ordering and the people making and delivering, need to take into account not only the physical demands of the identity programme, the colours, the logos, the typography, but also its demands in terms of quality. In practice, however, they rarely do.

This is the process that takes place. After the toiling and moiling of the first two stages, the outlines of the corporate identity programme are agreed. Then work starts simultaneously first on developing the various visual elements into an effective kit of parts, second on a detailed implementation schedule that indicates which parts of the organisation will get the identity programme when, and third on arrangements to release the information about the new identity both inside and outside the company.

Normally the design consultants put the finishing touches to the design scheme while a mixed team from the client organisation and the consultancy company deal with the other two matters. An implementation team is formed which works under the leadership of somebody whom the company will have appointed to look after the job. Ideally the implementation team will be composed of representatives of the design consultants and from the appropriate departments of the client organisation. Sometimes the company will have made a special appointment—a vice president of corporate design, or a corporate identity manager to lead the team. More likely though it will have lumbered the PRO or marketing manager with the job. In any case, it is the company's representative, whatever he is called, who, working with the design consultants, calculates in detail how the identity should be introduced, at what speed, over which areas and at what cost.

The implementation programme is worked out on the basis of a series of compromises between cost, speed, available resources, promotional possibilities, technical problems and political requirements. The job of the implementation team, working under the corporate identity manager, is to look at the visual elements—that is the brand and company names, corporate symbol, logo, colours and various alphabets—in relation to all of the visual manifestations of the company. He is also responsible for seeing that in all of these items the mood the company wants to produce is introduced. For the purpose of convenience the media in which the ingredients work can be broken down into a series of separate sections, which are:

Corporate paper
Signs
Vehicle identification
Uniforms
Advertising
Sales promotion material
Packaging design
Product design
Exhibitions
Environmental design

The implementation team has to examine ways of introducing the identity programme in two directions simultaneously: vertically down the various branches and divisions of the company, and horizontally across its various departments—transport, buildings, maintenance, personnel and so on. The team must examine how each unit within the organisation will need to use the identity. Naturally it will do this in conjunction with appropriate executives from each of the divisions involved. Decisions will be taken and recommendations made on the extent to which the new identity will affect each unit, on how much name changing is required, on the relationship between existing brands and brand images and the new identity, on the speed with which the new identity is to be manifested, and of course on how it's all going to be paid for and by whom.

All of these matters have to be discussed not only with each of the major units involved, but with those directing the company as a whole. In these matters a single company or division cannot take unilateral decisions, because what it does and when and how it does it will have an impact on the whole organisation.

For example, if it is decided to change some of the company names in the group, this may provide a platform to launch the group identity thoroughly and quickly. Although it might involve spending some money at the beginning, economies of bulk purchase could provide opportunities for cost saving.

So the decision about the way in which the scheme is introduced by each unit will depend on getting agreement for the whole programme.

A certain degree of ingenuity is required in getting a design programme off to a good start. There are a number of ways open: the introduction of the identity and its gradual implementation over a range of activities on a replacement basis has the merit that it is simple and relatively inexpensive, but it tends to lack impact, and it doesn't allow for a situation in which one unit emerges clearly and separately to set an example.

Another possibility, which is to take one unit, a discrete operation whose impact is in one place and is readily observable, is also sometimes appropriate. If the unit is run by someone who thoroughly understands the programme and is sympathetic to it or who happens to be in a commercial situation in which he badly needs it, the chances are that it will be carried forward with a flair and spirit which will go a long way towards setting standards.

Once the scheme has been introduced and it works and is seen to work, there should be no difficulty in maintaining momentum. After the main launch the implementation will be carried out according to a timetable, which will normally correspond to the standard repainting, renewal and refurbishing schedule the organisation maintains.

From the moment of the launch to the point when implementation is seen to be making substantial progress can be quite a long time; in a largish international company easily as much as three years. Naturally the time taken directly relates to the amount of enthusiasm and energy put behind the project, and this depends on the money and energy that is allocated to it. The size of the organisation and the system that is used to carry out the programme also affect speed.

The key in implementation, as in so many other activities, is enthusiasm. In the beginning, at the time of the launch—when it is all new and untested, when people aren't sure if they like it, if it will lose them business, if it will make them look stupid—many companies tend to draw back from implementing the programme.

This inbuilt resistance can often be considerable. Once the new identity is seen to be successful, however, the mood changes and everyone wants to do it. Weary old phrases like 'nothing succeeds like success' and 'everyone wants to jump on the bandwagon' spring to mind, but it is true that as soon as it is seen to work everyone wants it.

Over the years there have been a number of efforts to overcome the problem of the identity programme that gets dissipated and diluted in practice. Two methods have been tried, often in combination. The first method is to explain the objectives of the corporate identity in great detail and very carefully to everyone at all levels of the organisation. The second method is to prepare some detailed working documents for use by those who are going to implement the identity programme.

Before the implementation programme starts, everybody in the organisation has to be told why the scheme is being introduced, what its aims are, how it will be implemented, and how the process will affect them and their department.

The company internal magazine or newsletter is in some ways a good medium to announce and explain the identity, but it lacks the immediacy and the punch of a film or video tape, or even of slides. It may be better to make a slide presentation and in larger organisations perhaps a more sophisticated audio-visual presentation.

In any case, the film or video tape or magazine article must emphasise the fundamental reasons behind the change; it must not trivialise the programme by emphasising the new colours or symbols. It can show how the company's existing efforts internationally are dissipated; how it calls itself J Bloggs in England, Bloggotti in Italy, Nbloga in Kenya, Austroblog in Austria, the Bloggo Corporation in USA, Hispanoblog in Spain, and so on. It can show how this situation loses money and makes company interchange difficult. It can show other kinds of waste. It must relate the overall intention of the company to immediate moves like laying down standards for buildings, but of course it must also show what the new visual system will look like on a representative selection of items and talk about how the programme of implementation affects people.

In many cases the external launch of the identity is just as important as its presentation internally. Although the same visual material can be used, the text, or in the case of a film or video tape, the sound track, is likely to be different.

Suppliers, customers, journalists, financial institutions, trade unions, local government representatives, members of parliament may all be interested. The implementation of a new identity is an opportunity in a sense to re-launch the company—it doesn't come very often and it should certainly not be missed.

The launch of the identity is sometimes a worthwhile subject for advertising, although it is very often difficult to do this without oversimplifying and trivialising the issues: 'You knew us as J Bloggs & Co—now, because of our world-wide range of interests and to make it easier to recognise and remember us, we have become The Bloggo Corporation.' If you can't do better than this it's probably better to do nothing at all.

So far as the rest of the launch is concerned, any competent public relations man can make out a list of the things to do—client lunches or parties, press conferences—all of which will help the organisation to create the right climate for the change.

So much then for the launch of the identity, both internally and externally. The other problem, which is how to control the quality of the output, is also complex and difficult. In reality there is no ideal way. People have to police the work as well as they can.

A few years ago small handbooks incorporating the rules for using the visual elements of the corporate identity were sometimes produced. Each department commissioning work received a copy of this document. Naturally, corporate identity managers were anxious to show these books to their bosses.

So some of the little handbooks were made a bit more attractive when they were used for this purpose. From there it was only a small step to the full-blown lush design manual that is now apparently obligatory for most major identity programmes.

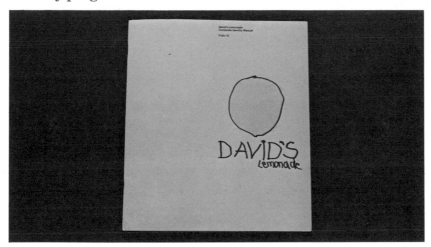

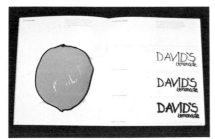

A manual gives even this spoof corporate identity programme the illusion of authority.

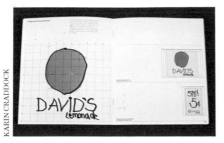

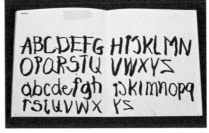

KARIN CRADDOCK

These purport to show suppliers of all kinds—signwriters, builders, architects, painters, vehicle suppliers, printers and advertising agents—how the design programme should be implemented across a wide range of subjects—letterheads, invoices, credit notes, sales brochures, technical brochures, packaging, advertising, buildings, internal signs, external signs, directional signs, location signs, colours of walls, ceilings, floors, upholstery and vehicles.

What is significant about these design manuals is that for the most part they are written and illustrated in such a way as to bear no relationship to reality at all. They are elaborate coffee-table productions enshrining for all time what the corporation wants to achieve, but not necessarily bearing much relationship to what has actually been or will be achieved.

The trouble with most design manuals is that in their attempts to enshrine what the corporate identity is all about they almost inevitably emphasise its mechanistic aspects at the expense of its ultimate intention. Although the design manual usually contains some kind of a preface from the chairman about the value of the corporate identity to the company, the bulk of the book shows obsessive concern for the minutiae and blinds everybody to what the programme is really there for.

The unfortunate fact is that for the most part the implementation of corporate identities is ineptly carried out. Even when the rules are strictly followed, which despite the manual is not always the case, the spirit of the corporate

KOKON CHUNG

HOMER SYKES

The manuals for British Rail's corporate identity (opposite) and (above and overleaf) the reality.

HOMER SYKES

identity is only too often ignored. If the newly painted vehicle is left to get filthy, if it is badly maintained so that its lights don't work properly, if its driver behaves offensively to other road-users, then the implementation programme might just as well not have taken place.

How can a well intentioned company get its implementation right? When a company gets the idea that design in which corporate identity plays a part is not some kind of desirable optional extra but has an intrinsic role to play in the organisation the appropriate mood has been created. When a company understands that its identity is perceived in everything it does and in how it does it, when in fact the spirit of the identity programme dominates the letter, a mood has been created in which constructive work can take place. This atmosphere favourable for the development of a corporate identity programme usually only exists when one man at the top realises its significance. Most companies are not dominated by one man with a restless spirit and a powerful propagandising mission; they are run by groups of people who spend most of their time compromising with others and the world outside to get what they hope is a little progress. Many people managing companies may be sympathetic to the principle of corporate identity, but in the nature of things few are going to be dedicated enthusiasts. For most executives and directors, however enlightened, it's just another management tool and one that they are unfamiliar with, can't evaluate, don't have experience of and are generally somewhat timid about.

Despite all this gloom, most of the companies that have instituted corporate identity programmes feel they have derived considerable benefit from them.

It would be unimaginable for Uniroyal to return to the days when its subsidiaries used different names in different countries and when it was bound so tightly to its origins. The corporate identity programme made it appear what it wanted to be, a truly international corporation.

Equally, it's impossible for BOC International to think of itself as it was before its new corporate identity took it away from the lumbering, staid, production-orientated world in which it had traditionally moved. BOC International's new corporate identity helped it to become the fast-thinking, fast-moving, confident, flexible group of companies struggling to fight its way out of the slow-moving giant.

Both of these companies gained a heightened sense of the possibilities open to them from their corporate identity programmes. Their corporate identities were an outward and visible sign of an internal commitment. In both of these examples the corporate identity is regarded by the management as a considerable success. But the management of these companies may be biased. To a considerable extent the people who commissioned the work, who were sold on the idea, who paid the money, are still running the show. Are there any more objective ways of checking how successful a corporate identity programme has been? What about research? Is there any image research technique that can enable a corporation to check on the impact, and perhaps even on the success, of its corporate identity programme?

It would be reassuring and comfortable to be able to say that there is, and that it works. It would induce a warm glow all round to be able to produce some examples of companies whose image ratings with various target groups (as they are so intriguingly called) measurably improved as their new corporate identities took root and emerged.

Unfortunately life, as usual, is not quite so tidy as one might wish. Of course there are many research companies who do work in this field, and some of these can produce case histories of organisations whose image has improved measurably as a result of this or that promotional exercise. Prestige advertising campaigns are often used as test beds for image research. It would be as glib and superficial to reject all image research as worthless as it would be to accept the extravagant and wholly unrealistic claims that are sometimes made for it. The facts of the matter are that nobody lives in isolation; great household names appear to us in a whole series of contexts every day of our lives. A prestige advertising campaign or a corporate identity programme for, say, ICI or Hoechst or Dupont and other great companies are only minor manifestations of the way in which they make an impact upon us. Products, packaging, trucks, news items, buildings, personal contacts, and perhaps above all these that immeasurable factor, word of mouth, rumour, all play a part over years and years in building or indeed in destroying a corporate reputation.

Even the image of companies whose contact with most people is minimal is powerfully affected by a combination of factors over which they have little control. Who can say whether and to what extent the Lockheed bribery scandals of 1976 have affected the company's reputation? Who can judge whether the McDonnell Douglas company has been badly crippled or hardly affected at all by the DC10

Turkish Airlines disaster at Paris in 1974? How much would a new corporate identity help Lockheed or McDonnell Douglas? How much would a prestige advertising campaign affect their imagery? Nobody can answer these questions with any degree of objectivity.

The corporate reputation is formed from the behaviour and performance of hundreds or thousands of people and products in an organisation. If a corporate identity is to be successful it will, over a considerable period of time, help to improve the performance of those thousands of people and products and to that extent, and only to that extent will its influence be measurable. Within this context research 'before' and 'after' the corporate identity programme is meaningless.

Anyway, what does a long period of time mean in this context? How long should a corporate identity last? Five years? Ten years? Forever? Should it ever be modified? Does it ever get out of date?

There are two factors that have an effect here: an outside and an inside dynamic. The first, the outside dynamic, is style, taste, mood, atmosphere, and this changes all the time, at certain times faster and more obviously, at other times more slowly. In visual terms tastes change: type styles, symbols and names go in and out of fashion, but moods change too. The current mood seems to run counter to big companies and multinationals, but 20, even 10 years ago size was encouraged, almost it seems for its own sake.

The second factor is the dynamic of the corporation itself. All corporations change, they grow by acquisition or they expand geographically, and they adopt new patterns of behaviour. Often they change quickly but relatively smoothly; sometimes, however, they change abruptly. A huge acquisition or a major divestment can have a profound effect on a company's centre of gravity and on its behaviour. It can turn a capital goods company into a consumer goods company, or the other way round.

It is impossible for any corporate identity, however carefully it has been conceived, to anticipate all of this. Inevitably opportunism and outside events will play a large part in determining the company's behaviour. Even among companies that stick to one or two things, say supermarket chains or banks, the corporate identity will inevitably need to be modified and kept up to date.

This does not mean that every two years, or for that matter every 20, a company needs to change its design style. What it does mean is that the way in which the identity is manifested—on packaging, in advertising, on signs, on buildings—should be regularly monitored and that it should be adapted and modulated when and where appropriate so that major changes are, if possible, obviated.

To take one example, the uniformity with which the major banks interpret their corporate identity is stiflingly unimaginative. Whether it's a village in Buckinghamshire, a major avenue in New York, an isolated town in Kenya or the High Street in Surbiton, Barclays, for example, grinds out the same boring mixture, no doubt labouring under the misapprehension that uniformity is what corporate identity is all about.

One day, no doubt sooner rather than later, Barclays and the others will find that the whole thing is out of date and inappropriate and each of them will have to start a new identity programme all over again. What Barclays and organisations like it should do is constantly monitor and, where necessary, modulate and modify, keeping the identity alive without destroying its basic disciplines.

Naturally there is a danger that the liberty to change with changing circumstances will degenerate into licence, and it is of course essential to get the right balance. There are many ways in which the monitoring of the identity and its adaptation when necessary can be carried out. Perhaps the most effective is one to which I referred earlier in another context: when a major new job, say a new building or the launch of a new piece of equipment, gives an opportunity for a significant appraisal or re-appraisal of the identity, that opportunity should be seized.

There is an essential difference between an active and a passive corporate identity. The passive identity is the classic house style—the symbol, the logotype and the alphabet—that has to be used in certain sizes and forms in a given set of circumstances and then forgotten forever.

The active corporate identity is the one that has a discipline and rules, but is open to wise interpretation by certain carefully authorised individuals or groups who are permitted, and in fact encouraged, to develop it.

This represents the difference between an intelligent understanding of identity as an active management tool and its passive and mechanistic use.

Postscript

Many books begin with some definitions. This book will end with a few.

The terminology used in the trade is for the most part loose and sloppy. The phrases corporate identity, corporate image, corporate personality, visual identity, house style, design scheme and visual programme are all used more or less interchangeably and indiscriminately by many people who talk and write about the subject, including no doubt myself.

Attempts to define the difference between corporate personality, corporate image and corporate identity have been for the most part trivial, arbitrary and pedantic. Nevertheless, a further effort must be made or we shall all continue to be unclear and imprecise, not just in how we refer to these things, but also in how we think about them.

There are genuine differences between all of these expressions, but they are for the most part differences of nuance and accent rather than of meaning. The confusion arises because the real depth of the subject is only beginning to be explored; consequently some people feel that corporate identity is a superficial activity, while others take the view that its implications are more profound.

My definitions relate largely to the depth in which the subject is perceived. I start with the term house style, which defines the subject at its most superficial level. A house style is a graphic design scheme applied to some, most or even all of a company's visible manifestations. House style to my mind implies a cosmetic job.

Corporate personality, on the other hand, embraces the subject at its most profound level. It is the soul, the persona, the spirit, the culture of the organisation manifested in some way. A corporate personality is not necessarily something tangible that you can see, feel or touch—although it may be.

The tangible manifestation of a corporate personality is a corporate identity. It is the identity that projects and reflects the reality of the corporate personality. Sometimes, as we know, the corporate identity is introduced as a catalyst to encourage the development of a corporate personality; sometimes it reflects not what is, but what the corporation would like to be. A corporate image is what people actually perceive of a corporate personality or a corporate identity.

If these definitions are accepted, all the others fall into place. A design scheme is a synonym for house style, sometimes used for rather small scale projects. A brand identity is the same as a corporate identity used in the context of a brand, but while a brand identity makes good sense, a brand personality is a contradiction in terms. No brand is profound or real enough to have a real personality.

As for the other phrases—visual identity, visual programme and so on—these are just alternative ways of saying or writing design scheme. So much then for definitions.

No doubt these tentative definitions will be challenged and superseded as the corporate identity business changes and develops. I anticipate that many other observations that I have made and conclusions that I have drawn will be similarly disputed and modified by other writers on the subject over the next few years.

To me one of the real excitements of corporate identity activity is that it is for the most part uncharted territory— that it is in a state of flux and change and that none of us knows quite how it will develop and what it will become. The only thing that seems clear is that it is a real growth business, and one in which I hope some of those who have read this book will in one way or another participate.

The publishers are grateful for permission to use extracts from the following sources.

The United States: a Companion to American Studies edited by Dennis Welland. Methuen & Co. Ltd.

Princes and Artists: Patronage and Ideology at Four Habsburg Courts 1517-1633 by Hugh Trevor-Roper. Thames & Hudson Ltd; USA Harper and Row.

Industry and Empire: an Economic History of Britain since 1750 by Eric Hobsbawm. Penguin Books Ltd.

The Age of Capital, 1848-1875 by Eric Hobsbawm. Weidenfeld & Nicolson Ltd.

London's Historic Railway Stations by John Betjeman. John Murray Ltd.

Inside the Third Reich by Albert Speer. Weidenfeld & Nicolson Ltd; USA Macmillan Inc.

The Seven Sisters: the Great Oil Companies and the World They Made by Anthony Sampson. Hodder & Stoughton Ltd.

The Economist 26 February 1977.

The Guardian 12 May 1977, article by James MacManus.

Truck January 1977.

The Sunday Times 3 April 1977.

Marcus Samuel, First Viscount Bearsted and Founder of the 'Shell' Transport and Trading Company, 1853-1927 by Robert Henriques. Barrie & Jenkins.

Pioneers of Modern Design by Nikolaus Pevsner. Penguin Books Ltd.

New York Magazine 26 January 1976.

LIBRARY, UNIVERSITY OF CHESTER